– CELEBRATING A –
Holy Catholic
Easter

— CELEBRATING A —

Holy Catholic Easter

A Guide to the Customs and Devotions of Lent
and the Season of Christ's Resurrection

Fr. William Saunders

TAN Books
Charlotte, North Carolina

Cover and interior design by Caroline K. Green

Library of Congress Control Number: 2019948696
ISBN: 978-1-5051-1421-8
Published in the United States by
TAN Books
PO Box 410487
Charlotte, NC 28241
www.TANBooks.com
Printed in the United States of America

To my dear mother,
Pauline C. Saunders,
whose favorite
holiday is Easter

Contents

Introduction

"Alleluia! Christ is risen!" was the greeting of the early Christians to one another on Easter Sunday morning, to which the response would be, "He is truly risen!" Easter is the most solemn and joyful celebration of the Church year. We celebrate with renewed faith that our Lord Jesus Christ suffered, died, and rose for our salvation. The Lord Jesus has conquered sin, suffering, death, and evil itself. Christ has triumphed, and we will share in his victory if we remain faithful. As St. Paul said, "If we have died with him / we shall also live with him; / if we persevere / we shall also reign with him" (2 Tm 2:11–12).

Unfortunately, Easter is overshadowed by our Christmas celebration. Perhaps it is because the Christmas marketing hype now begins in the fall, with the emphasis on gift giving and decorating. Instead of being a time of spiritual preparation, Advent has given way to parties and other celebrations. Since there seems to be more activity and excitement surrounding Christmas, the significance of Easter is lost for many people.

While Advent and Christmas focus on the birth of our Savior, Lent and Easter focus on our rebirth as children of God and members of the Church. Yes, Lent is a penitential season, but the lack of activity—the decorating, gift giving, and partying—is a great blessing. Lent provides the opportunity to focus on our relationship with the Lord Jesus and to grow spiritually through prayer, fasting, and sacrifice. Here is a time to open ourselves to abundant graces. If a person takes Lent seriously as a time of introspection and conversion, then Easter becomes a real celebration of a renewed faith in the love of God as shown us through our Savior, Jesus Christ.

Therefore, this book is meant to help individuals and families journey through Lent and to make it a time of spiritual renewal, and thereby to celebrate Easter as a rising to new life with the Lord. Then each of us can truly proclaim, "Alleluia! Christ is risen! And he has risen in my life!"

Lent

Preparing for Lent: Shrovetide

Shrovetide is the week preceding the beginning of Lent. The word itself, *Shrovetide*, is the English equivalent for the Italian *Carnivale*, which is derived from the Latin words *carnem levare*, meaning "to take away the flesh." (Note that in Germany, this period is called "Fasching," and in parts of the United States, particularly Louisiana, "Mardi gras.") While this was seen as the last chance for merriment, and unfortunately in some places has resulted in excess and debauchery, Shrovetide was the time to cast off the things of the flesh and prepare spiritually for Lent.

Actually, the English term provides the best meaning for this period. "To shrive" meant to hear the confession of the penitent sinner; that is, in hearing a confession, the priest was shriving the sinner. In the Anglo-Saxon "Ecclesiastical Institutes," recorded by Theodulphus and translated by Abbot Aelfric about AD 1000, Shrovetide was described as follows: "In the week immediately before Lent everyone shall go to his confessor and confess his deeds and the confessor shall so shrive him as he then may hear by his deeds what he is to do in the way of penance." To highlight the point and motivate the people, special plays or masques were performed which portrayed the passion of our Lord or final judgment. Clearly, this Shrovetide preparation for Lent included the confessing of sin and the reception of absolution; as such, Lent then would become a time for penance and renewal of faith.

One last point: When "carnivale" or "mardi gras" became for some people a debauched party, the Church tried to restore the penitential nature of this time. In 1748, Pope Benedict XIV instituted the "Forty Hours of Carnival," whereby prayers were offered and the Blessed Sacrament was exposed in churches during the three days preceding Ash Wednesday. In a letter entitled "Super Bacchanalibus," he granted a plenary indulgence to anyone who adored the exposed Blessed Sacrament by offering prayers and making atonement for sins.

Shrove Tuesday and Pancakes

While the week of Shrovetide condoned the partaking of pleasures from which a person would abstain during Lent, Shrove Tuesday had a special significance in England. In the Middle Ages, people abstained from all forms of meat and animal products (although some areas allowed for food like fish). For example, Pope St. Gregory (d. 604), writing to St. Augustine of Canterbury, issued the following rule: "We abstain from flesh, meat, and from all things that come from flesh, as milk, cheese, and eggs." So in England, pancakes were prepared and enjoyed because in so doing, a family depleted their eggs, milk, butter, and fat, all of which were part of the Lenten fast. Therefore, the eating of pancakes on Shrove Tuesday became a tradition. For this same reason, Easter was celebrated with decorated eggs and fresh breads.

Perhaps in our own day, during a hearty dinner of pancakes on Shrove Tuesday, the family could "strategize" on what they plan to do for Lent: What will each person give up as a sacrifice? What spiritual practices could be performed, like attending Stations of the Cross or praying the Rosary? When will they go for confession? Such a strategy will help each member and the family as a whole to enter into the spirit of Lent.

Lent: A Forty-Day Spiritual Journey

Lent is a special time of prayer, penance, sacrifice, and good works in preparation for the celebration of Easter. In the desire to renew the liturgical practices of the Church, *The Constitution on the Sacred Liturgy* of the Second Vatican Council stated, "The season of Lent has a twofold character: primarily by recalling or preparing for baptism and by penance, it disposes the faithful, who more diligently hear the word of God and devote themselves to prayer, to celebrate the paschal mystery. This twofold character is to be brought into greater prominence both in the liturgy and by liturgical catechesis" (no. 109). The word *Lent* itself derives from the Anglo-Saxon words *lencten*, meaning "spring," and *lenctentid*, which literally means not only "springtide" but also was the word for "March," the month in which the majority of Lent falls.

Since the earliest times of the Church, there is evidence of some kind of Lenten preparation for Easter. For instance, St. Irenaeus (d. 203) wrote to Pope St. Victor I commenting on the celebration of Easter and the differences between practices in the East and the West: "The dispute is not only about the day, but also about the actual character of the fast. Some think that they ought to fast for one day, some for two, others for still more; some make their 'day' last forty hours on end. Such variation in the observance did not originate in our own day, but very much earlier, in the time of our forefathers" (Eusebius, *History of the Church*, V, 24).

When Rufinus translated this passage from Greek into Latin, the punctuation made between "forty" and "hours" made the meaning to appear to be "forty days, twenty-four hours a day." The importance of the passage, nevertheless, remains that since the time of "our forefathers"—always an expression referring to the apostles—a forty-day period of Lenten preparation existed. However, the actual practices and duration of Lent were still not homogenous throughout the Church.

Lent became more regularized after the legalization of Christianity through the Edict of Milan in AD 313. The Council of Nicea (325), in its disciplinary Canons, noted that two provincial synods should be held each year, "one before the forty days of Lent." St. Athanasius (d. 373) in his "Festal Letters" implored his congregation to make a forty-day fast prior to the more intense fasting of Holy Week. St. Cyril of Jerusalem (d. 386) in his *Catechectical Lectures*, which are the paradigm for our current Rite of Christian Initiation for Adults programs, had eighteen pre-baptismal instructions given to the catechumens during Lent. St. Cyril of Alexandria (d. 444) in his series of "Festal Letters" also noted the practices and duration of Lent, emphasizing the forty-day period of fasting. Finally, Pope St. Leo (d. 461) preached that the faithful must "fulfill with their fasts the Apostolic institution of the forty days," again noting the apostolic origins of Lent. One can safely conclude that by the end of the fourth century, the forty-day period of Easter preparation known as Lent existed and that prayer and fasting constituted its primary spiritual exercises.

Of course, the number forty has always had special spiritual significance regarding preparation. On Mount Sinai, preparing

to receive the Ten Commandments, "Moses stayed there with the LORD for forty days and forty nights, without eating any food or drinking any water" (Ex 34:28). Elijah walked "forty days and forty nights" to the mountain of the Lord, Mount Horeb (another name for Sinai) (1 Kgs 19:8). Most importantly, Jesus fasted and prayed for "forty days and forty nights" in the desert before he began his public ministry (Mt 4:2).

Once the period of forty days of Lent was established, the next development concerned how much fasting was to be done. In Jerusalem, for instance, people fasted for forty days, Monday through Friday, but not on Saturday or Sunday, thereby making Lent last for eight weeks. In Rome and in the West, people fasted for six weeks, Monday through Saturday, thereby making Lent last for six weeks. Eventually, the practice prevailed of fasting for six days a week over the course of six weeks, and Ash Wednesday was instituted to bring the number of fast days before Easter to forty. Since Sunday is a solemnity when we celebrate the resurrection of the Lord, it is not included in the forty-day period of Lent, and, thus, one is not bound to observe fasting or abstinence.

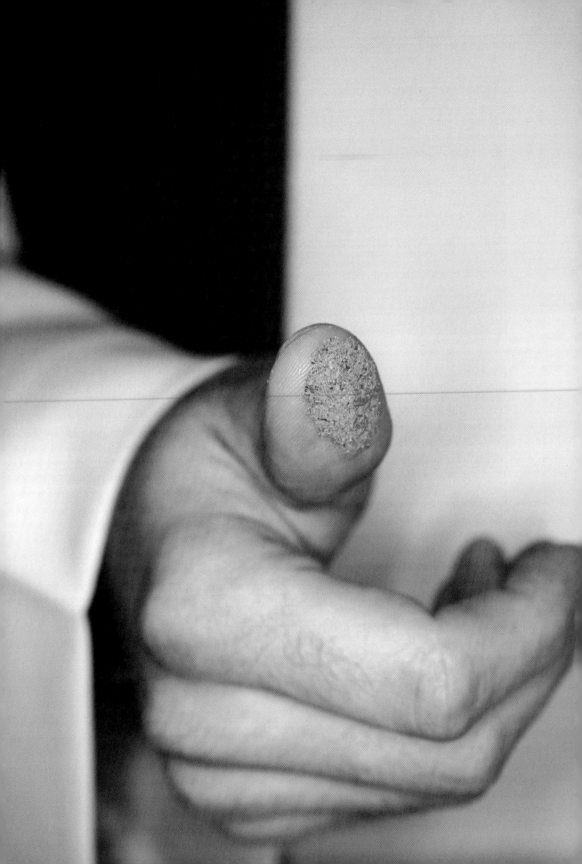

Why Ashes on Ash Wednesday?

The liturgical use of ashes originates in the Old Testament times. Ashes symbolized mourning, mortality, and penance. For instance, in the Book of Esther, Mordecai put on sackcloth and ashes when he heard of the decree of King Ahasuerus (or Xerxes, 485–464 BC) of Persia to kill all the Jewish people in the Persian Empire (see Est 4:1). Job (whose story was written between seventh and fifth centuries BC) repented in sackcloth and ashes (see Jb 42:6). Prophesying the Babylonian captivity of Jerusalem, Daniel (c. 550 BC) wrote, "I turned to the Lord God, pleading in earnest prayer, with fasting, sackcloth, and ashes" (Dn 9:3). In the fifth century BC, after Jonah's preaching of conversion and repentance, the town of Nineveh proclaimed a fast and put on sackcloth, and the king covered himself with sackcloth and sat in the ashes (see Jon 3:5–6). These Old Testament examples evidence both a recognized practice of using ashes and a common understanding of their symbolism.

Jesus himself also made reference to ashes: referring to towns that refused to repent of sin although they had witnessed the miracles and heard the good news, our Lord said, "If the mighty deeds done in your midst had been done in Tyre and Sidon, they would long ago have repented in sackcloth and ashes" (Mt 11:21).

The early Church continued the usage of ashes for the same symbolic reasons. In his book *De Poenitentia*, Tertullian (c. 160–220) prescribed that the penitent must "live without joy in the roughness of sackcloth and the squalor of ashes." Eusebius (c. 260–340), the famous early Church historian, recounted in his *The History of the Church* how an apostate named Natalis came to Pope Zephyrinus clothed in sackcloth and ashes begging forgiveness. Also during this time, for those who were required to do public penance, the priest sprinkled ashes on the head of the person leaving confession.

In the Middle Ages (at least by the time of the eighth century), those who were about to die were laid on the ground on top of sackcloth sprinkled with ashes. The priest would bless the dying person with holy water, saying, "Remember that thou art dust and to dust thou shalt return." After the sprinkling, the priest asked, "Art thou content with sackcloth and ashes in testimony of thy penance before the Lord in the day of judgment?" To which the dying person replied, "I am content." In all of these examples, the symbolism of mourning, mortality, and penance is clear.

Eventually, the use of ashes was adapted to mark the beginning of Lent. The ritual for the "Day of Ashes" is found in the earliest editions of the Gregorian Sacramentary, which dates at least to the eighth century. About the year 1000, an Anglo-Saxon priest named Aelfric preached, "We read in the books both in the Old Law and in the New that the men who repented of their sins bestrewed themselves with ashes and clothed their bodies with sackcloth. Now let us do this little at the beginning of our Lent that we strew ashes upon our heads to signify that we ought to repent of our sins during the Lenten fast."

As an aside, Aelfric reinforced his point by then telling of a man who refused to go to church on Ash Wednesday and receive ashes; the man was killed a few days later in a boar hunt. Since the Middle Ages at least, the Church has used ashes to mark the beginning of the penitential season of Lent, when we remember our mortality and mourn for our sins.

In our present liturgy for Ash Wednesday, we use ashes made from the burned palm branches distributed on the Palm Sunday of the previous year. The priest blesses the ashes using one of the two formulas:

O God, who are moved by acts of humility and respond with forgiveness to works of penance, lend your merciful ear to our prayers and in your kindness pour out the grace of your blessing on your servants who are marked with these ashes, that, as they follow the Lenten observances, they may be worthy to come with minds made pure to celebrate the Paschal Mystery of your Son. Through Christ our Lord. Amen.

Or

O God, who desire not the death of sinners, but their conversion, mercifully hear our prayers and in your kindness be pleased to bless these ashes, which we intend to receive upon our heads, that we, who acknowledge we are but ashes and shall return to dust, may, through a steadfast observance of Lent, gain pardon for sins and newness of life after the likeness of your Risen Son. Who lives and reigns for ever and ever. Amen.

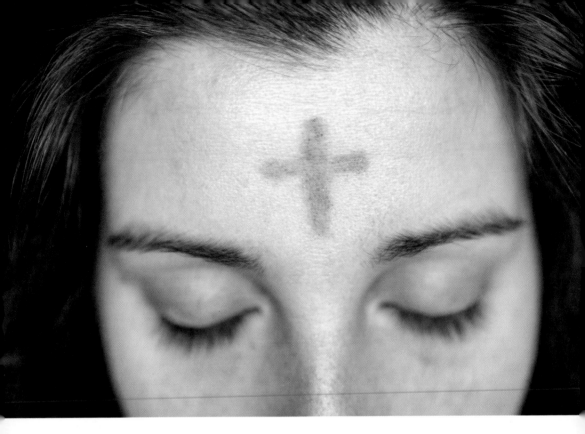

Having then sprinkled the ashes with holy water, the priest imposes them on the foreheads of the faithful, making the sign of the cross and saying, "Remember, that you are dust and to dust you shall return," or, "Repent, and believe in the Gospel."

Therefore, as we begin this holy season of Lent in preparation for Easter, we must remember the significance of the ashes we have received: We mourn and do penance for our sins. We again convert our hearts to the Lord, who suffered, died, and rose for our salvation. We renew the promises made at our baptism, when we died to an old life and rose to a new life with Christ. Finally, mindful that the kingdom of this world passes away, we strive to live the kingdom of God now and look forward to its fulfillment in heaven. In essence, we die to ourselves and rise to a new life in Christ.

In all, Lent reminds us of the great love God has shown to us through our Savior, Jesus Christ, and we are called to renew and grow in our love for him. We must open our hearts to the Holy Spirit and allow him to move us to charity toward our neighbors. Pope St. John Paul II, in his *Message for Lent*, 2003, said, "It is my fervent hope that believers will find this Lent a favorable time for bearing witness to the Gospel of charity in every place, since the vocation to charity is the heart of all true evangelization." He also lamented that our "age, regrettably, is particularly susceptible to the temptation toward selfishness which always lurks within the human heart. . . . An excessive desire for possessions prevents human beings from being open to their Creator and to their brothers and sisters." This Lent, acts of self-giving love shown to those in need must be part of our penance, conversion, and renewal, for such acts constitute the solidarity and justice essential for building up the kingdom of God in this world.

Prayer, Fasting, and Almsgiving

On Ash Wednesday, the priest proclaims the Lord Jesus's teaching found in the Gospel of St. Matthew (6:1–18) whereby the faithful are exhorted to pray, fast, and give alms. These three spiritual exercises constitute the three pillars of a good spiritual program or rule of life. In this way, not only are we encouraged to perform these exercises during Lent, but also use them as a paradigm of our spiritual life throughout the year. In a way, we could say, "Lent is a time to get our souls in shape," but in such a way as not to let them fall out of shape once Lent is over.

The *Catechism* highlights the importance of these three forms of penance, "which express conversion in relationship to oneself [fasting], to God [prayer], and to others [almsgiving]" (1434).

Prayer

Daily prayer is essential. The *Catechism* reads: "Great is the mystery of faith! . . . This mystery, then, requires that the faithful believe in it, that they celebrate it, and that they live from it in a vital and personal relationship with the living and true God. This relationship is prayer" (2558). The *Catechism* then quotes two great saints: First, St. Therese of Lisieux, who said, "For me, prayer is a surge of the heart; it is a simple look turned toward heaven, it is a cry of recognition and of love, embracing both trial and joy" (2558). Second, St. John Damascene, who said, "Prayer is the raising of one's mind and heart to God or the requesting of good things from God" (2559).

During Lent, and each day, a person needs to find fifteen minutes for prayer and fifteen minutes for spiritual reading. Why fifteen minutes? Author Matthew Kelly, in his book *The Four Signs of a Dynamic Catholic*, found 6.4 percent of registered parishioners contribute 80 percent of the volunteer hours in a parish; 6.8 percent of registered parishioners donate 80 percent of financial contributions; and there is an 84 pecrent overlap between the two groups (p. 12). He also found that the 7 percent category had two things in common: they spent an average of fifteen minutes in prayer each day (whether saying the Rosary, attending daily Mass, or some other devotion) and spent an average of fifteen minutes studying the faith each day—whether reading the *Catechism*, Sacred Scripture, or another book, or even watching or listening to spiritual CDs, DVDs, or other programs, like on EWTN (pp. 16–21).

Therefore, Lent offers a great opportunity to develop a "program of life." Here we punctuate the day with prayer. A possible paradigm would be as follows:

Make a morning offering. A person could say a formal prayer, like the Our Father; or an aspiration, like, "Good morning, Jesus. I love you," or, "Jesus, walk with me this day."

Another good prayer with which to start the day is the Guardian Angel prayer: "Angel of God, my guardian dear, to whom God's love commits me here. Ever this day be at my side, to light, to guard, to rule, and to guide."

Lastly, if a person is struggling with a particular weakness or temptation, and trying to overcome a habitual sin, asking the Lord for help at the beginning of the day brings great graces to strengthen us.

Offer grace before meals. Before eating, always pause to say the blessing. Even if at a restaurant, pausing to bow the head, make the sign of the cross, and say the blessing is a wonderful witness. If we are with others who may not be Catholic, we should not be inhibited from saying grace, whether inviting the others persons to participate or saying it privately by ourselves.

Schedule time for fifteen minutes for prayer and fifteen minutes of spiritual reading. Our lives have schedules and routines—from work, school, exercise, eating, and personal care. Schedule time for prayer and spiritual reading. Find a good time when the best attention can be given. If we wait until the end of the day, too often we are tired and only good for "horizontal meditation"; that is, sleep.

End the day with prayer. Before hitting the bed for the day, pause for prayer. Make a brief examination of conscience and then offer the Act of Contrition. Thank the Lord for the blessings of the day. Pray for the family and other loved ones. This prayer will help us rest with the Lord during the night.

Other options. While the foregoing has been a basic structure for prayer, a person can add on a daily basis the praying of the Angelus at noon or evening and praying the Rosary (especially during the official fifteen-minute period). Making a good confession is also essential. Monthly confession is recommended, and of course you must confess any grave sins before receiving Holy Communion. Attend daily Mass (even if only once a week), or make a visit to the Blessed Sacrament during the week. Also, praying the Stations of the Cross on Fridays, especially with the parish community, is both a great meditation and a penance.

Fasting

Fasting and abstinence also receive special emphasis during Lent. We are body and soul, and so fasting intensifies a physical dimension to our prayer: even though we may not be spiritually engaged in prayer, physically, we are praying through our fasting. Before he began his public ministry, our Lord was in the desert, where he fasted and prayed for forty days.

Fasting was part of penance: the Prophet Daniel fasted and prayed for his sins and the sins of the people, confessing, "We have sinned, been wicked and done evil; we have rebelled and departed from your commandments and your laws. We have not obeyed your servants the prophets, who spoke in your name to our kings, our princes, our fathers, and all the people of the land" (Dn 9:5–6).

Fasting is a powerful weapon against evil: when the apostles were not successful in exorcising a demon, Jesus said, "This kind does not come out except by prayer and fasting" (Mt 17:21).

Therefore, during Lent, each of us should undertake some form of fasting and abstinence and unite them to our prayer. Our fasting will intensify our prayer for a special intention; help atone for our sins, the sins of others, or the Poor Souls in purgatory; and be a weapon against the evils that confront us, inside and outside of the Church.

The original rules of fasting varied. First, some areas of the Church abstained from all forms of meat and animal products, while others made exceptions for food like fish. Second, the general rule was for a person to have one meal a day, in the evening or at three o'clock in the afternoon.

These Lenten fasting rules also evolved. Eventually, a smaller repast was allowed during the day to keep up one's strength for manual labor. Eating fish was allowed, and later eating meat was also allowed through the week except on Ash Wednesday and Friday. Dispensations were given for eating dairy products if a pious work was performed, and eventually this rule was relaxed totally.

Over the years, modifications have been made to the Lenten observances, making our practices not only simple but also rather easy. Ash Wednesday still marks the beginning of Lent which lasts for forty days, not including Sundays. The present fasting and abstinence laws are very simple: On Ash Wednesday and Good Friday, the faithful fast (having only one full meal a day and smaller snacks to keep up one's strength) and abstain from meat. On the other Fridays of Lent, the faithful abstain from meat. People are still encouraged "to give up something" for Lent as a sacrifice. An interesting note is that technically on Sundays and other solemnities like St. Joseph's Day (March 19) and the Annunciation (March 25), one is exempt and can partake of whatever has been offered up for Lent. Nevertheless, I personally believe that if you gave something up for the Lord, tough it out. Don't act like a Pharisee looking for a loophole.

Fasting, however, must be intentional, not just something done for Lent. The Lord spoke to the Prophet Isaiah, "Would that today you might fast so as to make your voice heard on high! . . . This, rather, is the fasting that I wish: releasing those bound unjustly, untying the thongs of the yoke; Setting free the oppressed, breaking every yoke; Clothing the naked when you see them, and not turning your back on your own. Then your light shall break forth like the dawn, and your wound shall quickly be healed" (Is 58:4–8). Here, the Lord is not saying that fasting by itself is useless, but it must be intentional to aid in our personal conversion.

As such, we should abstain from what controls us: If sweets are the craving, we abstain from them during Lent. If being tardy and keeping others waiting is the problem, we strive to be on time, even early. If being attached to video games, computer time, or television absorbs our attention, we give that time to prayer, like attending the Stations of the Cross, and doing good works, like helping more in the family or the parish. All of us can think of something with which we struggle or that has too much control over us. Through prayer and intentional fasting, a person can conquer vice and increase in virtue.

Almsgiving

While we think of almsgiving as giving money to those in need, we could broaden that to include giving of our time and talent, as well as our treasure. In our modern world, oftentimes the time and talent are more precious and harder to give to help others than the money. Also, the best and most worthy almsgiving is sacrificial, not giving from our surplus, but from our want, as described in the story of the Widow's Mite (see Lk 21:1–4).

The Old Testament provides a beautiful teaching on the importance of almsgiving: Tobit teaches his son, Tobiah:

Give alms from your possessions. Do not turn your face away from any of the poor, and God's face will not be turned away from you. Son, give alms in proportion to what you own. If you have great wealth, give alms out of your abundance; if you have but little, distribute even some of that. But do not hesitate to give alms; you will be storing up a goodly treasure for yourself against the day of adversity. Almsgiving frees one from death, and keeps one from going into the dark abode. Alms are a worthy offering in the sight of the Most High for all who give them. (Tb 4:7–11)

Later, the Archangel Raphael said to Tobit and Tobiah, "It is better to give alms than to store up gold; for almsgiving saves one from death and expiates every sin" (Tb 12:8–9). Finally, Sirach teaches, "Water quenches a flaming fire, and alms atone for sins" (Sir 3:29).

In the New Testament, our Lord frequently spoke of being generous. In the Sermon on the Mount, he said, "When you give alms, do not let your left hand know what your right hand is doing" (Mt 6:3). Too often, the "right hand" inspires a person to be generous in some way and then the "left hand" hesitates and dissuades him, saying, "You have already given so much. You have done enough. This is too much. Someone else will take care of it." Coincidentally, in Latin, *left* is "sinister" and *right* is "dexter."

As such, we can practice almsgiving in conjunction with our fasting or abstinence. For example, the money saved by not eating at restaurants, going to the movie theater, or eating desserts could be saved and, at the end of Lent, given to a particular charity or placed in the parish poor box. Closets and toy chests could be purged of old, forgotten, or seldom used items and given to charity. A visit and the offering of some refreshment could be made to an elderly person who is alone. All of these examples could be performed individually and as a family.

Beer and Pretzels

Beer and pretzels are the official beverage and food of Lent. (However, much of the information available is based on tradition that has been handed down through the ages.) In the early Church, the Lenten abstinence and fasting laws were stricter than what the faithful practice today, as we learned in the previous section. Recall, many areas of the Church abstained from all forms of meat and animal products, while others made exceptions for food like fish. The general rule was for a person to have one meal a day, in the evening or at three o'clock in the afternoon, and smaller snacks to maintain strength. So a need arose for simple food and drink which would fulfill the abstinence and fasting laws.

According to pretzel maker Snyder's of Hanover, a young monk in the early 600s in Italy was preparing a special Lenten bread of water, flour, and salt. To remind his brother monks that Lent was a time of prayer, he rolled the bread dough in strips and then shaped each strip in the form of crossed arms, mimicking the then popular prayer position of folding one's arms over each other on the chest. The three holes were said to represent the Holy Trinity—Father,

Son, and Holy Spirit—to whom all prayer is addressed. The bread was then baked as a soft bread, just like the big soft pretzels one can find today.

Because these breads were shaped into the form of crossed arms, they were called *bracellae,* the Latin word for "little arms." From this word, the Germans derived the word *bretzel,* which has since mutated to the familiar word *pretzel.*

Another possibility for the origins of the word *pretzel* is that the young monk gave these breads to children as a reward when they could recite their prayers. The Latin word *pretiola* means "little reward," from which *pretzel* could also be reasonably derived.

Apparently, this simple Lenten food became very popular. Pretzels were enjoyed by all people. They became a symbol of good luck, long life, and prosperity. Interestingly, they were also a common food given to the poor and hungry. Not only were pretzels easy to give to someone in need but also they were both a substantial food to satisfy the hunger and a spiritual reminder of a merciful God knowing a person's needs and answering our prayers.

Another interesting story involving pretzels arose when the Ottoman Turks were besieging the city of Vienna, Austria in 1529. The Turks could not break the city's defenses, so they began to tunnel below ground. The monks in the basement of the monastery were baking pretzels and heard the sound of digging. They alerted the guard and saved the city. As a sign of appreciation, the emperor gave to the monks their own pretzel coat of arms.

The soft pretzels eventually evolved into hard baked pretzels. Another story is that a young monk dozed off while tending to the oven where the pretzels were baking. As the oven fire began to die out, he awoke and stoked the oven. In the end, he had overbaked the pretzels. At first the master baker monk was upset, but soon discovered that the hard pretzels were also delicious. These hard pretzels were less perishable than the soft ones, and thereby easy to have available to give to the poor and hungry.

As an aside, in Bavaria and Austria, "Palm Pretzels" are baked for Palm Sunday. These can range in size from one foot to three feet, and weigh up to five pounds. In Luxembourg, on *Laetare Sunday* (the Fourth Sunday of Lent, the Sunday of Rejoicing), boys give pretzels to girls whom they like, and the size of the pretzel corresponds to how much the boy likes the girl. Then on Easter, the girl will give a decorated Easter egg to the boy if she wishes to show her interest in him.

So what about the beer to go with the pretzels? In the 1600s, the Minim Friars (the Order of Minims founded by St. Francis of Paola in the 1400s) established a new monastery—Coloister Neudeck ob der Au in Bavaria, near the city of Munich. They began brewing beer in 1634 and did so until 1799, when the monastery was closed. At that time, Franz Xavar Zacherl bought the brewery, and the Paulaner Brewery began production, following the monks' traditions.

Paulaner Brewery braumeister Martin Zuber explained that during Lent, the monks needed more than water (since they abstained from wine during Lent) and vegetables to sustain them. So they brewed a very strong beer, high in carbohydrates and nutrients. These were doppelbock beers, which are strong lagers with a heavy flavor and a color ranging from pale to amber to dark brown. They were also referred to as "a meal in a glass" or "liquid bread."

A tradition survives that the monks, fearing that their beer was too good and too enjoyable for Lent, decided to ask the Holy Father in Rome for a decision. They sent a barrel of their beer to Rome, but unfortunately it spoiled on the way. When the pope tasted it, he found it distasteful. He ruled that drinking it was a "sacrifice unto itself" and the monks were to be commended for making such sacrifice during Lent. Taking the ruling to heart, the monks named their beer "Sankt Vater" or "Holy Father's Beer." Even today, this beer is called "Salvator" and is still served at the annual Oktoberfest.

Interestingly, beer provides many positive health benefits: protein, B-complex vitamins, iron, magnesium, phosphorus, potassium, selenium, silicon, and antioxidants. The website *Organic Facts* also notes beer protects against heart disease, increases bone density, lowers risk of type-2 diabetes, prevents anemia, lowers

risk of gall stones and kidney stones, increases urination, increases good cholesterol (thereby reducing risk of dementia and heart disease), improves digestion, and reduces stress. In all, the monks knew what they were doing! And the beer and pretzels make for a more enjoyable Lent.

Stations of the Cross

Since Lent is a penitential season of preparation for Easter, the Stations of the Cross, which follow the path of Christ from Pontius Pilate's praetorium to Christ's tomb, have been a popular devotion in parishes. In the sixteenth century, this pathway was officially entitled the *Via Dolorosa* (Sorrowful Way), or simply the Way of the Cross or Stations of the Cross.

This devotion has evolved over time. Tradition holds that when our Blessed Mother lived in Jerusalem, she visited the scenes of our Lord's passion daily. After Constantine legalized Christianity in the year 312, this pathway was marked with its important stations. St. Jerome (342–420), living in Bethlehem during the latter part of his life, attested to the crowds of pilgrims from various countries who visited these holy places and followed the Way of the Cross.

This devotion continued to grow in popularity. In the fifth century, an interest developed in the Church to "reproduce" the holy places in other areas so pilgrims who could not actually travel to the Holy Land could do so in a devotional, spiritual way in their hearts. For instance, St. Petronius, bishop of Bologna (d. 450), constructed a group of chapels at the monastery of San Stefano which depicted the more important shrines of the Holy Land, including several of the stations. After the fall of Jerusalem in 637 to the invading Muslims, the resulting persecution of the Church and religious practices, as well as the hindering of pilgrimages, motivated the churches to erect the Stations of the Cross. Although the Crusaders were able to liberate the Holy Land for a short time, the Muslims regained control in 1183, and the persecution began again.

St. Francis of Assisi popularized the Stations. In 1219, he set sail to the Nile Delta to convert the Muslims. Meeting with Sultan Malek al-Kamil, St. Francis said, "If you and your people will accept the word of God, I will with joy stay with you. If you yet waver between Christ and Mohammed, cause a fire to be kindled [a bed of hot coals], and I will go into it with your priests that you may see which is the true faith." The imams refused, but St. Francis walked on the hot coal unharmed. Although genuinely moved, the sultan said that if he accepted Christianity, both he and St. Francis would be killed. Leaving disappointed, St. Francis was able to visit the Holy Places before returning to Italy. Nevertheless, St. Francis was inspired to promote the devotion to the passion of the Lord and the spiritual exercise of the Stations of the Cross. He is also credited with the phrasing at each station, "We adore you, O Christ, and we praise you. Because by your Holy Cross you have redeemed the world."

In 1342, the Franciscans were appointed as guardians of the shrines of the Holy Land. The faithful received indulgences for praying at the following stations: at Pilate's praetorium, where Christ met his mother, where he spoke to the women, where he met Simon of Cyrene, where the soldiers stripped him of his garments, where he was nailed to the cross, and where he was buried in the tomb.

At this time, the manner of praying the stations varied. William Wey, an English pilgrim, visited the Holy Land in 1458 and again in 1462, and he is credited with the term *stations*. He described the manner in which a pilgrim followed the steps of Christ. Prior to this time, the path usually followed the reverse course of ours today—moving from Mount Calvary to Pilate's praetorium. At this time, the reverse—going from Pilate's praetorium to Calvary—seems to have taken hold.

The number of stations has also varied. William Wey's account has fourteen stations, but only five correspond to our own. Some versions included the house of Dives (the rich man in the Lazarus story), the city gate through which Christ passed, and the houses of Herod and Simon the Pharisee. In 1584, a book written by

Adrichomius entitled *Ierusalem sicut Christi Tempore floruit* (*Jerusalem as It was in the Time of Christ*) gives twelve stations which match those in our present version. This book was translated into several languages and circulated widely. In the sixteenth century, devotional books appeared, especially in the Low Countries, which had fourteen stations with prayers for each one.

When the Turks blocked access to the Holy Land, reproductions of the stations were erected at popular spiritual centers, including the Dominican Friary at Cordova and the Poor Clare Convent of Messina (early 1400s); Nuremberg (1468); Louvain (1505); Bamberg, Fribourg, and Rhodes (1507); and Antwerp (1520). Many of these stations were produced by renowned artists and are considered masterpieces today.

By 1587, Giovanni Zuallardo, a sixteenth-century traveler and author, reported that the Muslims also forbade anyone "to make any halt, nor to pay veneration to [the stations] with uncovered head, nor to make any other demonstration," basically suppressing this devotion in the Holy Land. Nevertheless, the devotion continued to grow in popularity in Europe.

At the end of the seventeenth century, the erection of stations in churches became more popular. In 1686, Pope Innocent XI, realizing that few people could travel to the Holy Land due to the Muslim oppression, granted the Franciscans the right to erect stations in all of their churches and that the same indulgences would be given to the Franciscans and those affiliated with them for practicing the devotion as if on an actual pilgrimage. Pope Benedict XIII extended these indulgences to all of the faithful in 1726. Five years later, Pope Clement XII permitted stations to be erected in all churches and fixed the number at fourteen. In 1742, Pope Benedict XIV exhorted all priests to enrich their churches with the Way of the Cross, which must include fourteen crosses and are usually accompanied with pictures or images of each particular station. The popularity of the devotion was also encouraged by preachers like St. Leonard Casanova (1676–1751) of Porto Maurizio, Italy, who reportedly erected over six hundred sets of stations throughout Italy.

To date, there are fourteen traditional stations: Pilate condemns Christ to death; Jesus carries the cross; the first fall; Jesus meets his blessed Mother; Simon of Cyrene helps carry the cross; Veronica wipes the face of Jesus; the second fall; Jesus speaks to the women of Jerusalem; the third fall; Jesus is stripped of his garments; Jesus is nailed to the cross; Jesus dies on the cross; Jesus is taken down from the cross; and Jesus is laid in the tomb. Because of the intrinsic relationship between the passion and death of our Lord with his resurrection, several of the devotional booklets now include a fifteenth station which commemorates the Resurrection.

Take advantage of this beautiful devotion individually, as a family, or with a congregation. A plenary indulgence is granted for those who piously exercise the Way of the Cross, actually moving from station to station where they are legitimately erected and while mediating on the passion and death of our Lord (*Enchiridion of Indulgences*, no. 63). Those who are impeded from visiting a church may gain the same indulgence by piously reading and meditating on the passion and death of our Lord for half an hour. Pope St. John Paul II prayed the Stations of the Cross every Friday, as best he could. A wise religious sister friend of mine, Sr. Mary Joan, IHM, who was so kind to me in seminary and who has now gone to the Lord, always said, "As I pray the stations, I see my own life and know Jesus is walking with me."

Confession: Why and How

Sometimes people—Catholics and non-Catholics alike—ask, "Why do you have to confess your sins to a priest? Why can't I just ask God for forgiveness?" We confess to the priest for three reasons: First, Christ himself instituted this sacrament, just as he instituted the other six sacraments. The priest has the authority of the apostles by virtue of his ordination to absolve sins in the name of the Lord. On the night of the Resurrection, Jesus said to the apostles, "Receive the Holy Spirit. Whose sins you forgive are forgiven them, and whose sins you retain are retained" (Jn 20:22–23). The priest is the minister of the sacrament acting in the person of Christ. If confession were not a sacrament instituted by our Lord which conveys grace, I would be the first to say, "Go, see your counselor, therapist, or psychiatrist." Instead, because Christ gave the Church this sacrament of forgiveness, I preach, "Go to confession. Receive the graces that forgive, heal, and strengthen." Ironically, those who sometimes resist confession have no difficulty asking the priest to come for the "Last Rites."

Second, the priest is the spiritual father. Just as we see a doctor for healing when we are physically sick, we see a priest when our soul is sick and needs healing. To take the priest-doctor analogy further, just as a person becomes nervous visiting a doctor or may be anxious over what a doctor may find or prescribe, that same person knows the doctor's guidance will bring better health; the same is true with the spiritual medicine a priest has to offer.

Third, the priest represents the Church and the people we have sinned against. Yes, sin offends Almighty God, but sin also affects our neighbors. In the early days of the Church, people publicly confessed their sins at the beginning of Mass and were absolved. Much to our relief, this practice was changed to the Penitential Rite we have now at Mass, and private confession was instituted.

Now, for the "How?" Really, the "how to make a good confession" has not really changed. Granted, the Second Vatican Council did decree that "the rite and formulas for the sacrament of penance are to be revised so that they more clearly express both the nature and effect of the sacrament" (*Sacrosanctum Concilium*, no. 72). Accordingly, the Sacred Congregation for Divine Worship issued *The Rite of Penance* in 1973. The new rite did add options for prayers, provide for a reading of Sacred Scripture, and introduce parish "penance services" with private confessions. Nevertheless, the norms stipulated, "It is for priests, and especially parish priests in reconciling individuals or the community, to adapt the rite to the concrete circumstances of the penitents" (*The Rite of Penance*, no. 40). Therefore, on a Saturday afternoon with a line of penitents waiting for confession, the parish priest may follow a more streamlined version of the rite, which would include by custom the traditional format for confession.

With that in mind, a person begins with a good examination of conscience. We need to hold up our life to the pattern of life God has revealed for us to live through our Savior, Jesus Christ. For instance, we take time to reflect on the Ten Commandments, the Beatitudes, the precepts of the Church, the cardinal virtues (prudence, fortitude, temperance, and justice), and the seven capital sins (pride, anger, envy, gluttony, sloth, lust, and covetousness). We recognize both the sins of commission as well as omission. (Several versions of an examination of conscience are available in pamphlet form or on websites. One also follows in the next section.)

The examination of our conscience is like stepping back and looking at the picture of our life in comparison to the masterpiece of life revealed by God. Remember, when we were children, we used to trace pictures. Tracing helped us learn to draw. We would take a piece of plain paper, hold it over the original picture, and then put it up to the window. The light would enable us to trace the original picture onto our blank sheet of paper. Periodically, we had to stop and step back to see if our paper had slipped and was out of kilter with the original, or if we had deviated from the lines.

In a similar way, as we live our lives, we are tracing them in accord with God's pattern of life. In examining our consciences, we step back and honestly assess how well we fit God's pattern and have stayed within his boundaries. At this time, we reflect on the progress we have made since our last confession in dealing with weaknesses, faults, temptations, and past sins. Hopefully, we see improvement in our spiritual well-being.

However, when we have gone out of kilter or deviated from God's masterpiece, we have sinned, perhaps not just by commission, but also by omission. In other words, we can sin by failing to do good as much as we can by doing something bad. That said, we must distinguish the venial sins (those lighter sins which weaken our relationship with the Lord) from the mortal sins (those sins which sever our relationship with the Lord and "kill" the presence of sanctifying grace in our souls). A good priest can help us do that if we are unsure ourselves. Here we remember the words of Jesus, "Everyone who does wicked things hates the light and does not come toward the light, so that his works might not be exposed. But whoever live the truth comes to the light, so that his works might be clearly seen as done in God" (Jn 3:20–21).

Given this examination of conscience, we have contrition for our sins. While we are sorry for sin because we do fear the fires of hell and the loss of heaven, and the just punishments of God, we are sorry most of all because our sins offend God whom we should love above all things. The love for God moves us to repent of sin and seek reconciliation. All of the great saints regularly examined their consciences and made frequent use of the sacrament of Penance. Pope St. John Paul II confessed his sins at least weekly, as did St. Teresa of Calcutta. One must ask, "Why? What sins did these holy people possibly commit?" They loved the Lord so much that even the slightest omission or commission moved them to confession. They did not want even the slightest sin to separate them from the love of God. For love of God, we too are sorry for our sins. The more we love, the more we are moved to sorrow for sin, even venial sin.

Sorrow for sin moves us to have a firm amendment not to sin again. We probably will sin again, but we try not to do so. We do not plan on leaving the confessional and committing the same sins again. We proceed to confession with a humble and contrite heart, and with the desire to become a saint.

We then confess our sins. When we enter the confessional in most churches, we have the option of remaining anonymous or facing the priest. Whichever option a person chooses, always remember that whatever is said during the confession, the priest must hold in secret. He can never break the seal of confession.

We proceed by making the sign of the cross and saying, "Bless me, Father, for I have sinned." One could also simply begin, "In the name of the Father . . ." We should then state when we made our last confession: "It has been (so long) since my last confession."

We then confess our sins. We must be specific. Sometimes people say, "I broke the sixth commandment," which covers everything from a lustful thought to pornography and adultery. We do not need to provide the full-blown story with every detail; rather, we present just the basics to enable the priest to help. If he needs clarification, he will ask. We need to give some quantification; for example, missing Mass once is different from several times which is different from all the time. When we are finished confessing our sins, we state, "I am sorry for these and all of my sins."

With this information, the priest may counsel us. He may also ask questions, like, "Do you pray each day? Do you attend Mass every Sunday?" to make sure we are in good spiritual health. He also assigns a penance for the healing of the hurt caused by sin and the strengthening of our soul against future temptation. In many ways, the priest is like a medical doctor who needs enough information to diagnose the problem, assess the state of health, and prescribe a regimen for good health, except the priest is a spiritual doctor. He deals in souls.

He then asks us to say an act of contrition, which is generally the traditional prayer: "Oh my God, I am heartily sorry for having offended thee. I detest all of my sins because of thy just punishments, but most of all because they offend thee, my God, who art all good and deserving of all of my love. I firmly resolve with the help of thy grace to sin no more and to avoid the near occasions of sin. Amen."

Finally, the priest imparts absolution. Ponder the beautiful words: "God the Father of mercies, through the death and resurrection of His Son, has reconciled the world to Himself and sent the Holy Spirit among us for the forgiveness of sins; through the ministry of the Church may God give you pardon and peace, and I absolve you from your sins, in the name of the Father, and of the Son, and of the Holy Spirit." This formula emphasizes our merciful heavenly Father, the saving mystery of our Lord's passion, death, and resurrection, and the healing ministry of the Holy Spirit through the Church. Can we not hear the very words of Jesus: "God so loved the world that he gave his only Son, so that everyone who believes in him might not perish but might have eternal

life. For God did not send his Son into the world to condemn the world, but that the world might be saved through him" (Jn 3:16–17)? Meditating upon these words, can we not picture the Blood of Jesus, the Lamb of God, pouring forth from his Sacred Heart, cleansing us and washing us clean?

The priest then dismisses us, saying, "Give thanks to the Lord, for he is good," to which we respond, "His mercy endures forever."

(Many priests may simply say, "May God bless you" or "Go in peace.") We then leave the confessional to do the assigned penance.

The sacrament of Penance is a beautiful sacrament through which we are reconciled to God, ourselves, and our neighbors. Remember the words of St. Paul, "God, who is rich in mercy, because of the great love he had for us, even when we were dead in our transgressions, brought us to life with Christ" (Eph 2:4–5). Take time to make a good confession during Lent.

Making a Good Examination of Conscience

A good examination of conscience must begin with remembering who God is and our relationship to him. In his first epistle, St. John taught, "God is love" (1 Jn 4:8), and he has shown his love perfectly through his Son, our Savior Jesus Christ: "In this is love: not that we have loved God, but that he has loved us and sent his Son as expiation for our sins" (1 Jn 4:10). Therefore, St. John continued, "Our fellowship is with the Father and with his Son, Jesus Christ" (1 Jn 1:3). Through Baptism, we became a child of God and have been identified as a Christian and a member of the Catholic Church (see 1 Jn 1:2).

To live in that love, we must follow the commandments. Jesus said, "As the Father loves me, so I also love you. Remain in my love. If you keep my commandments, you will remain in my love, just as I have kept my Father's commandments and remain in his love" (Jn 15:9–10).

Pope Benedict XVI, in his homily for the Feast of the Baptism of the Lord (2006), summarized this teaching well and set the foundation for a good examination of conscience:

Baptism inserts us into communion with Christ and therefore gives life. . . .

. . . But a gift must be accepted, it must be lived.

A gift of friendship implies a *yes* to the friend and a *no* to all that is incompatible with this friendship, to all that is incompatible with the life of God's family, with true life in Christ. . . .

We might also say that the Face of God, the content of our great *yes*, is expressed in the Ten Commandments, which are not a pack of prohibitions, of *noes*, but actually present a great vision of life.

They are a *yes* to God who gives meaning to life (the first three Commandments); a *yes* to the family (Fourth Commandment); a *yes* to life (Fifth Commandment); a *yes* to responsible love (Sixth Commandment); a *yes* to solidarity, to social responsibility, to justice (Seventh Commandment); a *yes* to the truth (Eighth Commandment); a *yes* to respect for others and for their belongings (Ninth and Tenth Commandments).

This is the philosophy of life, the culture of life that becomes concrete and practical and beautiful in communion with Christ, the living God, who walks with us in the companionship of his friends, in the great family of the Church.

Let's now proceed with a good examination of conscience by reflecting on each of the Ten Commandments.

FIRST COMMANDMENT: I am the Lord your God. You shall not have strange gods before me.

Do I love God with my whole heart, mind, soul, and strength?

Do I place God first in my life, making him the top priority?

Have I taken good time to pray each day, to read Sacred Scripture or other spiritual reading, to say grace before meals?

Have I allowed anything to become a false god or an idol in my life, consuming my attention and becoming the first priority over God, spouse, or family (e.g., money, popularity, social status, power, and the like)?

Have I ever received Holy Communion in the state of mortal sin?

Have I told a lie when making a confession, and, thus, deliberately deceived the priest?

Have I rejected any of the teachings of the Church?

Have I been involved with superstitious practices or things of the occult, like fortune tellers, mediums, Ouija boards, tarot cards, voodoo, and the like?

Have I wished evil on someone or commanded God to damn another person?

SECOND COMMANDMENT: You shall not take the name of the Lord your God in vain.

Have I used the name of the Lord, in particular the holy name of Jesus, in an expression of anger and in a careless way?

Have I used bad language, profanities, or curse words?

Have I blasphemed by joking about or mocking God, the Blessed Mother Mary and the saints, holy beliefs?

Have I profaned or abused a holy object?

Have I made any rash, false, or unnecessary oaths?

THIRD COMMANDMENT: Remember to keep holy the Lord's Day.

Have I attended and worshipped at Holy Mass on Sundays and Holy Days of Obligation?

Have I deliberately missed Holy Mass on Sundays and Holy Days of Obligation (e.g., skipping Mass because of sports, a social engagement, inconvenience, or laziness)?

Have I been reverent at Holy Mass?

Do I try to keep Sunday as truly "the Day of the Lord," taking time for Holy Mass, personal prayer, rest, relaxation, and family time?

FOURTH COMMANDMENT: Honor your father and your mother.

Have I given honor and due respect to my parents? Have I obeyed their legitimate rules and requests? Have I shared in the family responsibilities and chores and performed them cheerfully? Have I been mindful of the needs of my family members and offered assistance?

Have I cared for my elderly relatives, especially parents and grandparents?

Have I given honor to my vocation by praying with my children each day and teaching them the faith?

Have I respected all who have legitimate authority over me (e.g., employers, teachers, civil authorities, and law enforcement officials)? Have I obeyed just laws?

Have I respected my spiritual Father (i.e., my pastor)?

FIFTH COMMANDMENT: You shall not kill.

Do I respect and defend the sanctity of human life from conception until natural death?

Have I physically harmed someone, or even murdered someone?

Have I had an abortion, or encouraged or helped someone else to obtain one?

Have I promoted, encouraged, or directed an act of euthanasia?

Have I harmed myself by abusing alcohol or drugs, or by overeating or not getting proper rest?

Have I harmed myself through an act of mutilation (e.g., sterilization or personal harm)?

Have I spiritually harmed those entrusted to my care, especially my children, by not praying with them, not instructing them in the faith, or not taking them to Holy Mass each Sunday and Holy Day of Obligation?

Have I killed someone spiritually through anger or through harsh words, including gossip, slander, and detraction?

Have I harbored a grudge and hatred for a person in my heart? Have I refused to forgive a person?

Have I scandalized anyone, causing that person to sin or shaking that person's faith?

Have I jeopardized my well-being by associating with those who would tempt me to spiritual or physical harm?

SIXTH COMMANDMENT: You shall not commit adultery.

Do I respect and defend the dignity of the person, the sanctity of human sexuality, and the sanctity of marital (conjugal) love? Do I model my own life after the Blessed Mother Mary and St. Joseph?

Have I been unfaithful in my marriage and committed adultery?

Have I been chaste in my thoughts, words, and actions? Have I tried my best to dispel lustful thoughts?

Have I engaged or indulged in pornography?

Have I committed masturbation?

Have I committed fornication, having sexual relations outside of marriage?

Have I engaged in homosexual activity?

Have I used contraceptives or other methods that are not open to life?

Have I used fertility treatments that violate the unitive and procreative aspects of marriage and are condemned by the Church?

Have I dressed modestly? Have I been modest in speech? Have I been overly or inappropriately flirtatious?

SEVENTH COMMANDMENT: You shall not steal.

Have I striven to be just and fair in all of my dealings with others?

Have I respected the physical and intellectual property of others?

Have I stolen, vandalized, or destroyed the property of others?

Have I cheated or plagiarized?

Have I performed an honest day's work for an honest day's pay?

Have I shared my goods with those in need? Have I supported my Church and charitable institutions? Remembering the abundant blessings the Lord has given to me, do I tithe?

Have I wasted anything (e.g., food, time, or talents)?

EIGHTH COMMANDMENT: You shall not bear false witness against your neighbor.

Have I always spoken the truth, or have I lied or kept silent when I should have spoken?

Have I broken a confidence?

Have I deceived someone else?

Have I been prudent in speech, or have I gossiped or spread rumors about others?

Have I reported a wrong or a crime to proper authorities?

NINTH AND TENTH COMMANDMENTS: You shall not covet your neighbor's wife. You shall not covet your neighbor's goods.

Have I been envious or jealous of my spouse or someone else's spouse?

Have I been envious or jealous of someone else's possessions, abilities, attributes, or friendships?

Am I dissatisfied with my life, always looking back and thinking, "What if . . ." or looking around and thinking, "If only I . . ."?

Making a good examination of conscience is quite humbling, but also liberating. By recognizing our weaknesses and sins, we can then receive the graces of forgiveness and healing through the sacrament of Penance and renew our friendship with the Lord and our commitment to holiness. St. John admonished, "If we say, 'We have fellowship with him,' while we continue to walk in darkness, we lie and do not act in truth. . . . If we say, 'We are without sin,' we deceive ourselves, and the truth is not in us. If we acknowledge our sins, he is faithful and just and will forgive our sins and cleanse us from every wrongdoing. If we say, 'We have not sinned,' we make him a liar, and his word is not in us" (1 Jn 1:6–10).

The Solemnity of St. Joseph, March 19

March 19 marks the Solemnity of St. Joseph, technically a holy day of obligation recognized in traditionally Catholic countries, but dispensed in more secular countries, like the United States. Being a solemnity, the Gloria and Creed are prayed at Mass, and the faithful are dispensed from keeping their Lenten penances. We must rejoice this day and celebrate this holy and great man.

What We Know of St. Joseph and Why He Is Essential in the Life of Our Lord

St. Joseph truly is the silent figure of the New Testament. For instance, the Gospel does not record one spoken verse for St. Joseph. Nevertheless, what this great saint did for God in his life speaks volumes. To appreciate him and his role in salvation, we need to glean things from the Gospels of St. Matthew and St. Luke. St. Joseph was "of the house and family of David" (Lk 2:4). Because of this ancestry, St. Joseph is the linkage between the old covenant made with Abraham and Moses and the new, perfect, and everlasting covenant which will be made through the blood of Jesus. He brings to a close the notion of the Patriarch's promised land and King David's established kingdom and prepares the way for Jesus, the Messiah, who will establish the new kingdom of God and the new Promised Land—not a kingdom of land, castles, and armies, but a spiritual kingdom of truth, love, justice, and peace. The kingdom of God established by Jesus is not confined to this physical world but is a spiritual one that is within oneself; it is shared life with the Lord, lived now, and will be fulfilled in heaven.

St. Matthew identified St. Joseph as "an upright man." The original text is better translated as *just* or *righteous* (in Hebrew, *zadik*), which better reflects that he lived by God's standard, keeping the commandments and emulating God's love. For example, Abraham was "righteous," the spiritual father of the Jewish people, he whom we recognize as "our father in faith" (*Roman Canon* of the Mass).

St. Joseph was selected to be the foster father of our Lord. In the infancy account of the Gospel of St. Matthew, we read of how he was betrothed, or engaged, to Mary. Keep in mind that Jewish marriages—even for Orthodox Jews today—occurred in two distinct phases: The first phase was the *kiddushin*, or betrothal, when the groom and bride exchanged vows. They were now legally considered married. However, they still did not yet live together; the woman continued to live with her parents.

The second phase was the *nusuin*, which usually occurred after a year. With a bridal party of groomsmen, the husband would go to the home of his wife's family, where she and her bridesmaids would be waiting. He would bring her to his home to consummate the marriage, and they would live together as husband and wife for the rest of their lives. (This tradition is the basis for the parable of the five foolish bridesmaids in Matthew 25). Keep in mind, therefore, that Joseph and Mary are married at the time of the Annunciation, even though both are virgins.

In the Gospel, Joseph learned Mary was with child. He must have been heartbroken, wondering both how this happened and what he was supposed to do. He knew Mary was most holy. However, he also knew the child was not his, and, therefore according to the Torah, the marriage contract was broken. Technically, in such a case, Mary could have been stoned to death in the public square for infidelity (cf. Dt 22). Instead of pursuing such a juridic act, he chose quietly to divorce her—to break the contract—and let her go.

Nevertheless, the Angel of the Lord (presumably St. Gabriel) appeared to him in a dream, revealed to him that Mary had conceived by the power of the Holy Spirit, and commanded that he take Mary as his wife and Jesus as his own Son. Without question or hesitation, Joseph did as the angel commanded. Pope Benedict XVI, in his *Jesus of Nazareth: The Infancy Narratives*, provides a beautiful meditation on this scene:

> Once again this shows us an essential quality of the figure of Saint Joseph: his capacity to perceive the divine and his ability to discern. Only a man who is inwardly watchful for the divine, only someone with a real sensitivity for God and His ways, can receive God's message in this way. And an ability to discern was necessary in order to know whether it was simply a dream or whether God's messenger had truly appeared to him and addressed him.
>
> The message conveyed to Joseph is overwhelming, and it demands extraordinarily courageous faith. Can it be that God has really spoken, that what Joseph was told in the dream was

the truth—a truth so far surpassing anything he could have fore-seen? Can it be that God has acted in this way toward a human creature? Can it be that God has now launched a new history with men? Matthew has already said that Joseph "inwardly con-sidered" (*enthymethentos*) the right way to respond to Mary's pregnancy. So we can well imagine his inner struggle now to make sense of this breathtaking dream message: "Joseph, son of David, do not be afraid to take Mary your wife, for that which is con-ceived in her is of the Holy Spirit" (Matthew 1:20). (pp. 41–42)

Here again, we see the important role of Joseph: He is to take Jesus as his own Son and to name him, thereby giving him legal recogni-tion and legal personhood.

Please note that the foregoing understanding of the annuncia-tion is the traditional one. Some individuals have speculated that Joseph knew that Mary had conceived by the power of the Holy Spirit and thereby felt unworthy, even afraid, to marry her and accept this responsibility; therefore, he decided to divorce her qui-etly. However, if he already knew what had happened, why then would the angel later tell him in the dream that Mary had conceived by the power of the Holy Spirit? The traditional understanding is still the best one, and is supported by Pope Benedict XVI.

St. Joseph fulfilled his obligations with great fortitude. Through-out the Gospel, he faithfully and unquestioningly obeyed the com-mands of God: taking his family to the safety of Egypt to flee the wrath of King Herod, returning to Nazareth, presenting his child in the Temple for circumcision and formal presentation, and trav-eling to Jerusalem to celebrate Passover.

He accepted the responsibility of his vocation—being the faith-ful spouse of Mary and the foster father of Jesus. He provided the best he could for his family, whether in the stable, in Bethlehem,

or at home in Nazareth. Although the Gospels recount hardly any information about the Holy Family's life in Nazareth, they were people of modest means: when Joseph and Mary presented Jesus at the Temple, they offered two turtle doves as a sacrifice, an exception made for poorer families who could not afford the usual offering of a lamb.

To provide for his family, Joseph worked as a carpenter. The original word in the Gospel is *tekton*, which means "craftsman" or "artisan," thereby suggesting that he could well have been a builder of homes as well as a carpenter. As a good Jewish father, Joseph passed this trade onto his Son, and indeed Jesus is known as "the carpenter's son" (Mt 13:55) and "the carpenter" (Mk 6:3).

Although Joseph was not the physical father of Jesus, he was a *father* in every other sense of the word. At the time of the circumcision, eight days after the birth of our Lord, he would have held baby Jesus in his arms as the rabbi performed the sacred ritual. When asked, "What is the child's name?" he would have replied, "His name is Jesus." Without St. Joseph, Jesus would have been a bastard child who had no standing in either Jewish or pagan Roman society. Also, as a good Jewish father, he was responsible for the religious education of his Son, including teaching him to read, so that he could read the Sacred Scriptures.

Finally, Jesus must have loved and respected Joseph and Mary very much, for the Gospel reads, after the finding in the Temple, Jesus returned to Nazareth and "was obedient to them" (Lk 2:51). In all, St. Joseph selflessly set aside his own needs for the good of his family.

Moreover, Joseph must have been a fine, masculine example for Jesus considering that God, the Father, had entrusted his Son to his care. Archbishop Fulton Sheen, in his book *The World's First Love*, posited:

Joseph was probably a young man, strong, virile, athletic, handsome, chaste, and disciplined, the kind of man one sees . . . working at a carpenter's bench. Instead of being a man incapable of loving, he must have been on fire with love. . . . Young girls in those days, like Mary, took vows to love God uniquely, and so did young men, of whom Joseph was one so preeminent as to be called the "just." Instead then of being dried fruit to be served on the table of the King, he was rather a blossom filled with promise and power. He was not in the evening of life, but in its morning, bubbling over with energy, strength, and controlled passion. (pp. 77–78)

Tradition holds that Joseph died before Jesus began his public ministry. This belief is based on two points: first, he never appeared during the public ministry as did Mary,—at the wedding feast at Cana, for example—and second, from the cross, Jesus entrusted the care of his mother to St. John the Apostle, indicating she was a widow with no other children to care for her. Tradition also holds that he died in the presence of Jesus and Mary. For this reason, St.

Joseph is the patron saint of a holy death. Although not defined by the Magisterium, St. Francis de Sales (d. 1622) believed that St. Joseph was assumed body and soul into heaven:

> What is there left for us to say now if not that, in no way must we doubt that this glorious saint enjoys much credit in Heaven in the company of the One who favored him so much as to raise him there, body and soul; something which is all the more likely since we have no relic of him here below on earth. It seems to me no one can doubt this truth; for how could he have refused this grace to St. Joseph, he who had been obedient at all times in his entire life? (*Complete Works*)

The Testimony of Saints and Popes

Besides the aforementioned, other great saints have held great devotion to St. Joseph. St. Bernardine of Siena (d. 1444) preached, "He was chosen by the eternal Father as the trustworthy guardian and protector of His greatest treasures, namely, His divine Son and Mary, Joseph's wife. He carried out this vocation with complete fidelity until at last God called him, saying, 'Good and faithful servant, enter into the joy of your Lord.'"

St. Teresa of Avila (d. 1582), in her *Life*, wrote:

> I took St. Joseph as my advocate and protector, and recommended myself very earnestly to him. He came to my help in the most visible manner. This loving father of my soul, this beloved protector, hastened to pull me out of the state in which my body was languishing, just as he snatched me away from greater dangers of another nature which were jeopardizing my honor and my

eternal salvation! For my happiness to be complete, he has always answered my prayers beyond what I had asked and hoped for. I do not remember even now that I have ever asked anything of him which he has failed to grant. I am astonished at the great favors which God has bestowed on me through this blessed saint, and at the perils from which he has freed me, both in body and in soul.

Popes through the ages of the Church have also recognized the importance of St. Joseph. Pope Pius IX declared him the patron of the Catholic Church (1870). Pope Leo XIII, in *Quamquam Pluries* (1889), wrote, "Joseph was the guardian, the administrator and the legitimate and natural defender of the divine household of which he was the head. It was thus natural and very worthy of St. Joseph that, as he supported in another era all the needs of the Family of Nazareth which he wrapped in his holy protection, he now covers with his heavenly patronage and defends the Church of Jesus Christ" (no. 3). Pope Pius XI preached on St. Joseph's Feast Day in Rome, 1937, "He belongs to the working-class, and he bore the burdens of poverty for himself and the Holy Family, whose tender and vigilant head he was. To him was entrusted the Divine Child when Herod loosed his assassins against Him. In a life of faithful performance of everyday duties, he left an example for all those who must gain their bread by the toil of their hands. He won for himself the title of "The Just" serving thus as a living model of the Christian justice which should reign in social life" (*Divini Redemptoris*, no. 81). Pope John Paul II, in *Redemptoris Custos* (1989), exhorted the faithful to look to St. Joseph in our troubled age:

This patronage must be invoked, and it is always necessary for the Church, not only to defend it against dangers ceaselessly cropping up, but also and above all to support it in those fearful efforts at evangelizing the world, and spreading the new evangelization among nations where the Christian religion and life were formerly the most flourishing, but are now put to a difficult test. . . . May St. Joseph become for all a singular master in the service of the saving mission of Christ that is incumbent on each and every one of us in the Church: To spouses, to parents, to those who live by the work of their hands or by any other work, to persons called to the contemplative life as well as to those called to the apostolate. (no. 29)

Lastly, St. Joseph has been honored in our liturgy. Since the legalization of Christianity in AD 313, a Mass has been offered in his honor, beginning in the East. Pope St. John XXIII in 1962 ordered St. Joseph's name inserted into the Roman Canon (Eucharistic Prayer I), as did Pope Francis in 2013 for the other Eucharistic Prayers, a proper recognition for the Guardian of the Universal Church. Moreover, St. Joseph's feast day of March 19 is a solemnity and traditionally a holy day of obligation throughout the universal Church (*Code of Canon Law*, no. 1246); however, the United States was granted an exemption from the requirement at the request of the Third Plenary Council of Baltimore (1884) because of the difficulty of observing holy days in a non-Catholic environment.

In 1955, Pope Pius XII established the Feast of St. Joseph the Worker on May 1 to present St. Joseph as the exemplar of all working people and to focus on the true dignity of human labor in contrast to the May Day celebrations of communist countries.

St. Bernadine's Sermon

There is a general rule concerning all special graces granted to any human being. Whenever the divine favor chooses someone to receive a special grace, or to accept a lofty vocation, God adorns the person chosen with all the gifts of the Spirit needed to fulfill the task at hand.

This general rule is especially verified in the case of Saint Joseph, the foster-father of our Lord and the husband of the Queen of our world, enthroned above the angels. He was chosen by the eternal Father as the trustworthy guardian and protector of his greatest treasures, namely, his divine Son and Mary, Joseph's wife. He carried out this vocation with complete fidelity until at last God called him, saying: "Good and faithful servant, enter into the joy of your Lord."

What then is Joseph's position in the whole Church of Christ? Is he not a man chosen and set apart? Through him and, yes, under him, Christ was fittingly and honorably introduced into the world. Holy Church in its entirety is indebted to the Virgin Mother because through her it was judged worthy to receive Christ. But after her, we undoubtedly owe special gratitude and reverence to Saint Joseph.

In him the Old Testament finds its fitting close. He brought the noble line of patriarchs and prophets to its promised fulfillment. What the divine goodness had offered as a promise to them, he held in his arms.

Obviously, Christ does not now deny to Joseph that intimacy, reverence and very high honor which he gave him on earth, as a son to his father. Rather we must say that in heaven Christ completes and perfects all that he gave at Nazareth.

Now we can see how the last summoning words of the Lord appropriately apply to Saint Joseph: "Enter into the joy of your Lord." In fact, although the joy of eternal happiness enters into the soul of a man, the Lord preferred to say to Joseph: "Enter into joy." His intention was that the words should have a hidden spiritual meaning for us. They convey not only that this holy man possesses an inward joy, but also that it surrounds him and engulfs him like an infinite abyss.

Remember us, Saint Joseph, and plead for us to your foster-child. Ask your most holy bride, the Virgin Mary, to look kindly upon us, since she is the mother of him who with the Father and the Holy Spirit lives and reigns eternally. Amen. (Sermo 2, de S. Joseph: Opera 7, 16, 27–30)

The St. Joseph's Table

According to long-standing tradition, the St. Joseph's Altar or Table originated in Sicily during the early Middle Ages. Drought had struck the island. The crops had failed. The dried-out wheat stalks cracked beneath the feet of the poor farmers as they walked through their barren fields. Only a sea of dust and withered vines remained from what had once been row upon row of brightly colored fruits and vegetables. The people were starving.

And so, the people prayed. They implored the help of Saint Joseph, the holy foster father of Jesus, our Savior, and the guardian of the Holy Family, for relief from the terrible drought and famine. Finally, their prayers were answered. The heavens opened, and rain poured down, quenching the earth with saving, life-giving water. The people rejoiced.

After the new harvest, the grateful people prepared a special table to honor St. Joseph with assorted produce and special foods they had prepared. After offering their prayers of thanksgiving, they celebrated, enjoying their special foods. Afterwards, they distributed the food to the less fortunate.

Since then, the faithful have continued to honor St. Joseph on his Feast Day by erecting a table and celebrating through prayer and festivity. Of course, over time, the tables have become more elaborate and bountiful.

One piece of folklore, however, tells that the fava bean was the only crop which survived the drought. Being high in protein, these beans saved many people from starvation. The faithful also attributed this meager yet nutritious ration to the intercession of St. Joseph.

Whether the table is in a home or a church, is simple or ornate, small or large, the purpose is to honor this holy man who provided for his family, Jesus and Mary, and to ask for his protection and support for our own families. The only guidance for erecting a table is to arrange the tables in the shape of a cross and have three levels for the Holy Trinity. White table cloths cover the table. A statue of St. Joseph holding Baby Jesus adorns the top level. On the other levels, statues of our Blessed Mother Mary and other saints may be placed. Lit candles and also flowers, particularly the lily (representative of St. Joseph's purity), may also decorate the table. Some people even place pictures of deceased relatives on the table, mindful of St. Joseph being the patron of a holy death. Another possibility is to have a box in which people may place the personal petitions they have written, asking for St. Joseph's help. Lastly, the different pastries, cookies, and breads, and wine are placed on the table. The congregation or family then gathers around to conduct a short prayer service and blessing, which then leads to the festivity of honoring St. Joseph. One last point: after the celebration, some of the bounty is taken to the poor, the homebound, or those alone.

St. Joseph's Table Prayer Service

The following is a prayer service used at Our Lady of Hope Catholic Church in Potomac Falls, Virginia, which may be adapted for the needs of a family if the parish does not offer one. A group of families could also gather to celebrate this event. Whatever else we do this day, we must joyfully celebrate the Solemnity of the Guardian of our Savior and the Spouse of our Blessed Mother, St. Joseph.

OPENING PRAYER

Priest: In the name of the Father, and of the Son, and of the Holy Spirit.

All: Amen.

Priest: Let us pray.

Heavenly Father, today we honor the memory of Saint Joseph, guardian of Your Son, husband of the Virgin Mary, and patron of the Universal Church. We rejoice at his table, which is a sign of God's generous blessings and of our call to serve those entrusted to our care, and the poor and hungry. Through the intercession of Saint Joseph, may we join the saints at your banquet in the heavenly kingdom.

All: Amen.

Priest: The Lord be with you.

All: And with your spirit.

Priest: A reading from the Holy Gospel according to St. Matthew:

Now this is how the birth of Jesus Christ came about. When his mother Mary was betrothed to Joseph, but before they lived together, she was found with child through the Holy Spirit. Joseph, her husband, since he was a righteous man, yet unwilling to expose her to shame, decided to divorce her quietly. Such was his intention when, behold, the angel of the Lord appeared to him in a dream and said, "Joseph, son of David, do not be afraid to take Mary as your wife into your home. For it is through the Holy Spirit that this child has been conceived in her. She will bear a son and you are to name him Jesus, because he will save his people from their sins." All this took place to fulfill what the Lord had said through the prophet: "Behold, the virgin shall be with child and bear a son, and they shall name him Emmanuel," which means "God is with us." The Gospel of the Lord.

All: Praise be to you, Lord Jesus Christ.

A short homily or reflection may follow.

GENERAL INTERCESSIONS

Priest: We call upon the name of the Lord and ask the intercession of Saint Joseph as we present these petitions:

Reader: For each of us, that following the example of Saint Joseph, patron of the universal Church, we will strive always to build up the Body of Christ. Let us pray to the Lord.

All: Lord, You are our hope and our strength.

Reader: Saint Joseph, teach us to love and honor each member of our families with the love and reverence you had for Jesus and Mary. Let us pray to the Lord.

All: Lord, You are our hope and our strength.

Reader: For the continued growth and success of our parish, aided by the intercession of Saint Joseph. Let us pray to the Lord.

All: Lord, You are our hope and our strength.

Reader: Lord Jesus, You built Your own house upon rock; strengthen our Church in firm faith and unshakeable trust in You. Let us pray to the Lord.

All: Lord, You are our hope and our strength.

LITANY OF SAINT JOSEPH

Priest:	**All:**
Lord, have mercy	Lord, have mercy
Christ, have mercy	Christ, have mercy
Lord, have mercy	Lord, have mercy
God our Father in heaven	have mercy on us
God the Son, Redeemer of the world	have mercy on us
God the Holy Spirit	have mercy on us
Holy Trinity, one God	have mercy on us
Holy Mary	pray for us
Saint Joseph	pray for us
Noble son of the House of David	pray for us
Light of patriarchs	pray for us
Husband of the Mother of God	pray for us
Guardian of the Virgin	pray for us
Foster father of the Son of God	pray for us
Faithful guardian of Christ	pray for us
Head of the Holy Family	pray for us
Joseph, chaste and just	pray for us
Joseph, prudent and brave	pray for us
Joseph, obedient and loyal	pray for us
Pattern of patience	pray for us
Lover of poverty	pray for us
Model of workers	pray for us
Example to parents	pray for us
Pillar of family life	pray for us
Comfort of the troubled	pray for us
Hope of the sick	pray for us
Patron of the dying	pray for us
Terror of evil spirits	pray for us
Protector of the Church	pray for us
Lamb of God, You take away the sins of the world	have mercy on us
Lamb of God, You take away the sins of the world	have mercy on us
Lamb of God, You take away the sins of the world	grant us peace

Priest: Gathering our prayers as one, we pray to the Father in the words our Savior taught us:

All: Our Father . . .

PRAYER OF BLESSING

Priest: All provident God, the good things that grace this table remind us of Your many good gifts.

> Bless this food, and may the prayers of Saint Joseph, who provided bread for Your Son and food for the poor, sustain us and all our brothers and sisters on our journey towards Your heavenly kingdom.

> We ask this through Christ, our Lord

All: Amen.

SAINT JOSEPH'S PRAYER

Dear St. Joseph, you were entrusted with the care of Mary and our Savior Jesus Christ. You lived your vocation as a spouse and father with total faith, self-sacrificing love, and unwavering hope. Even in the midst of great trials and difficulties, you never hesitated in serving the Lord. For good reason, you have been declared the guardian of the family and the universal Church.

I implore your help. Beg of your Son the grace to live my vocation fully, and to face the trials and difficulties of life, so that I may see the hand of God in all that I do and never lose hope. Guide my parish along the path of righteousness. Inspire me and each member to serve the Lord generously. Help us to build a home in honor of our Blessed Mother, Mary, Our Lady of Hope, where your Son will be adored in the Blessed Sacrament and worshiped in the Holy Sacrifice of the Mass.

St. Joseph, I trust in you!

CONCLUDING RITE

Priest: Lord, you have given us the saints as our intercessors in heaven. May the prayers of Saint Joseph always help us to do Your will and live in Your love.

Grant this through Christ, our Lord.

All: Amen.

Priest: And may Almighty God bless you all, the Father, and the Son, and the Holy Spirit.

All: Amen.

Priest: Go in peace.

All: Thanks be to God.

The Solemnity of the Annunciation, March 25

On March 25, nine months before Christmas, the faithful celebrate the Solemnity of the Annunciation. We remember how the Archangel Gabriel was sent by Almighty God to announce to the Blessed Virgin Mary that she had been prepared and chosen to be the mother of our Savior. She had been conceived and born without Original Sin. So the Archangel Gabriel greeted her, "Hail, favored one! The Lord is with you." And then he said, "Do not be afraid, Mary, for you have found favor with God. Behold, you will conceive in your womb and bear a son, and you shall name him Jesus. He will be great and will be called Son of the Most High" (Lk 1:28, 30–32).

Having given her consent, "I am the handmaid of the Lord. May it be done to me according to your word" (Lk 1:38), Mary conceived by the Holy Spirit. Through her, Jesus, true God and Second Person of the Holy Trinity, entered this world becoming also true man. As St. John wrote, "The Word became flesh and

CELEBRATING A HOLY CATHOLIC EASTER

made his dwelling among us, and we saw his glory, the glory of the Father's only Son, full of grace and truth" (Jn 1:14).

The message of the Gospel is summarized in the Collect of the Mass: "O God, who willed that your Word should take on the reality of human flesh in the womb of the Virgin Mary, grant, we pray, that we, who confess our Redeemer to be God and man, may merit to become partakers even in His divine nature. Who lives and reigns with you in the unity of the Holy Spirit, one God, forever and ever."

While not a holy day of obligation, the faithful are encouraged to attend Mass on this great feast day celebrating the mystery of the Incarnation. Although March 25 falls during Lent, being a solemnity, the Gloria and Nicene Creed are prayed during the Mass. Also, during the Creed, the faithful kneel at the words, "and by the Holy Spirit was incarnate of the Virgin Mary, and became man."

Being a solemnity, the faithful are also encouraged to celebrate. Therefore, they are dispensed from their Lenten penances and sacrifices. However, I encourage families to pray the Joyful Mysteries of the Rosary and the Angelus.

A Meditation from Pope St. Leo the Great

Lowliness is assured by majesty, weakness by power, mortality by eternity. To pay the debt of our sinful state, a nature that was incapable of suffering was joined to one that could suffer. Thus, in keeping with the healing that we needed, one and the same mediator between God and men, the man Jesus Christ, was able to die in one nature, and unable to die in the other.

He who is true God was therefore born in the complete and perfect nature of a true man, whole in his own nature, whole in ours. By our nature we mean what the Creator had fashioned in us from the beginning, and took to himself in order to restore it.

For in the Saviour there was no trace of what the deceiver introduced and man, being misled, allowed to enter. It does not follow that because he submitted to sharing in our human weakness he therefore shared in our sins.

He took the nature of a servant without stain of sin, enlarging our humanity without diminishing his divinity. He emptied himself; though invisible he made himself visible, though Creator and Lord of all things he chose to be one of us mortal men. Yet this was the condescension of compassion, not the loss of omnipotence. So he who in the nature of God had created man, became in the nature of a servant, man himself.

Thus the Son of God enters this lowly world. He comes down from the throne of heaven, yet does not separate himself from the Father's glory. He is born in a new condition, by a new birth.

He was born in a new condition, for, invisible in his own nature, he became visible in ours. Beyond our grasp, he chose to come within our grasp. Existing before time began, he began to exist at a moment in time. Lord of the universe, he hid his infinite glory and took the nature of a servant. Incapable of suffering as God, he did not refuse to be a man, capable of suffering. Immortal, he chose to be subject to the laws of death.

He who is true God is also true man. There is no falsehood in this unity as long as the lowliness of man and the pre-eminence of God coexist in mutual relationship.

As God does not change by his condescension, so man is not swallowed up by being exalted. Each nature exercises its own activity, in communion with the other. The Word does what is proper to the Word, the flesh fulfils what is proper to the flesh.

One nature is resplendent with miracles, the other falls victim to injuries. As the Word does not lose equality with the Father's glory, so the flesh does not leave behind the nature of our race.

One and the same person—this must be said over and over again—is truly the Son of God and truly the son of man. He is God in virtue of the fact that "in the beginning was the Word, and the Word was with God, and the Word was God." He is man in virtue of the fact that "the Word was made flesh, and dwelt among us." (Epistle 28 ad Flavianum 3-4: PL 54, 763-767)

The Angelus

A beautiful prayer to be recited individually or as a family on the Solemnity of the Annunciation is the Angelus. This prayer evolved from the practice of reciting the Hail Mary three times in a row, a practice encouraged by St. Anthony of Padua (d. 1231).

St. Bonaventure (d. 1274), at a Chapter of the Order of the Friars Minor in 1269, proposed that the friars pray the three Hail Marys after Compline in the evening (the last prayer for the day of the Liturgy of the Hours). Here they would also meditate on the mystery of the Incarnation. The ringing of the bell would precede the recitation so that all of the friars and faithful would know it was time to pause and pray the three Hail Marys. This practice spread throughout the Church, and the actual ringing became known as "the Ave bell."

By the 1400s, the practice included a recitation in the early morning and noontime, as well as evening. Pope Sixtus IV in 1475 granted an indulgence for the recitation of the Angelus at noontime, and this was extended by Pope Leo X to the recitation of it at early morning and evening. A person still receives a partial indulgence for the recitation of the Angelus (*Enchiridion of Indulgences*, no. 9). Eventually, the standard practice was to ring "the Ave bell" with three sets of three rings each at 6 a.m., noon, and 6 p.m., again marking times for the recitation of the three Hail Marys and the recitation of the Divine Office.

The present form of the Angelus appeared in the late 1500s in *The Little Office of the Blessed Virgin Mary* (printed in Rome with the approval of Pope St. Pius V) and the *Handbook for Catholics*, written by St. Peter Canisius. The prayer is as follows:

V. The Angel of the Lord declared unto Mary.

R. And she conceived of the Holy Spirit.

Hail Mary . . .

V. Behold the handmaid of the Lord.

R. Be it done unto me according to your word.

Hail Mary . . .

V. And the Word was made flesh,

R. And dwelt among us.

Hail Mary . . .

V. Pray for us, O holy Mother of God,

R. That we may be worthy of the promises of Christ.

Let us pray. Pour forth, we beseech you, O Lord, thy grace into our hearts: that we, to whom the Incarnation of Christ, thy Son, was made known by the message of an Angel, may by his Passion and Cross be brought to the glory of his Resurrection. Through the same Christ our Lord. Amen.

On the Solemnity of the Annunciation, the family could gather in the evening before dinner or at bedtime prayers to recite the Angelus together. With the father taking the lead, the mother and children could respond. Also, one child could even be "the ringer," the one who rings the bell in three sets of three rings.

Lady's Day

In parts of Europe, the Solemnity of the Annunciation is called "Lady's Day." Since this was about the time when farmers would begin sowing seeds in the fields, they would ask our Blessed Mother's intercession for a successful growing season and harvest.

In central European countries, farmers would place a picture of the Annunciation in the barrel that held the seeds. They would then recite a prayer-rhyme, like this one from Austria:

O Mary, Mother, we pray you;
Your life today with fruit was blessed:
Give us the happy promise too,
That our harvest will be of the best.
If you protect and bless the field.
A hundredfold each grain must yield.
Saint Gabriel to Mary flies:
This is the end of snow and ice.

In Russia, a priest would bless the "Annunciation Bread," large wafers of wheat flour (like the hosts used for Mass and similar to the Polish oplatek), and give them to the faithful. Returning home, the father would break the wafer and give a piece to each of the family members and others present, like farm hands. They received it with a deep bow and ate it in silence. They then took the crumbs and buried them in the fields as a protection against drought, hail, frost, or other inclement weather.

Families who enjoy gardening can easily follow the Russian practice of sharing bread together and then placing a piece in the garden. They could also sprinkle the garden with Holy Water, asking for our Blessed Mother's protection of the flowers or vegetables during the upcoming growing season.

Another option for celebrating the Solemnity of the Annunciation comes from Sweden. In Swedish, Our Lady's Day is *Varfrudagen*, which is similar to Waffle Day, *Vaffeldagen*. Therefore, both Catholics and Lutherans (the state church of Sweden) celebrate this day by enjoying waffles, a practice easily adapted for a family dinner.

Mother of Sorrows

Since the Solemnity of the Annunciation occurs in proximity of Holy Week, a good meditation would be on our Blessed Mother under the title "Our Lady of Sorrows." This title focuses on her intense suffering and grief during the passion and death of our Lord. Traditionally, this suffering was not limited to just this event; rather, it comprised "the seven dolors" or "seven sorrows" of Mary, which were foretold by the Priest Simeon who proclaimed to Mary, "This child [Jesus] is destined for the fall and the rise of many in Israel, and to be a sign that will be contradicted (and you yourself a sword will pierce) so that the thoughts of many hearts may be revealed" (Lk 2:34–35). These seven sorrows of our Blessed Mother included the prophecy of Simeon, the flight of the Holy Family into Egypt, the loss and finding of the child Jesus in the Temple, Mary's meeting of Jesus on his way to Calvary, Mary's standing at the foot of the cross when our Lord was crucified, her holding of Jesus when he was taken down from the cross, and then our Lord's burial. The prophecy of Simeon that a sword would pierce our Blessed Mother's heart was fulfilled in these events. For this reason, Mary is sometimes depicted with her heart exposed and with seven swords piercing it. More importantly, each new suffering was received with the courage, love, and trust that echoed her *fiat*, "Let it be done unto me according to thy word," first uttered at the Annunciation.

This Feast of Our Lady of Sorrows grew in popularity in the twelfth century, although under various titles. Granted, some writings would place its roots in the eleventh century, especially among the Benedictine monks. By the fourteenth and fifteenth centuries, the feast and devotion were widespread throughout the Church.

Interestingly, in 1482, the feast was officially placed in the Roman Missal under the title of "Our Lady of Compassion," highlighting the great love our Blessed Mother displayed in suffering with her Son. The word *compassion* derives from the Latin roots *cum* and *patior*, which means "to suffer with." Our Blessed Mother's sorrow exceeded anyone else's since she was the mother of Jesus, who was not only her Son but also her Lord and Savior; she truly suffered with her Son. In 1727, Pope Benedict XIII placed the Feast of Our Lady of Compassion in the Roman Calendar on the Friday before Palm Sunday. This feast was suppressed with the revision of the calendar published in the *Roman Missal* of 1969.

In 1668, the feast in honor of the Seven Dolors was set for the Sunday after September 14, the Feast of the Holy Cross. The feast was inserted into the Roman calendar in 1814, and Pope Pius X fixed the permanent date of September 15 for the Feast of the Seven Sorrows of the Blessed Virgin Mary (now simply called the Feast of Our Lady of Sorrows). The key image here is our Blessed Mother standing faithfully at the foot of the cross with her dying Son: the Gospel of St. John recorded, "When Jesus saw his mother and the disciple there whom he loved, he said to his mother, 'Woman, behold, your son.' Then he said to the disciple, 'Behold, your mother'" (Jn 19:26–27). The Second Vatican Council in its *Dogmatic Constitution on the Church* wrote, "She stood in keeping with the divine plan, suffering grievously with her only-begotten Son. There she united herself, with a maternal heart, to His sacrifice, and lovingly consented to the immolation of this Victim which she herself had brought forth" (no. 58).

St. Bernard (d. 1153) wrote, "Truly, O Blessed Mother, a sword has pierced your heart. . . . He died in body through a love greater than anyone had known. She died in spirit through a love unlike any other since His" *(De duodecim praerogatativs BVM)*.

Focusing on the compassion of our Blessed Mother, Pope St. John Paul II, reminded the faithful:

Mary Most Holy goes on being the loving consoler of those touched by the many physical and moral sorrows which afflict and torment humanity. She knows our sorrows and our pains, because she too suffered, from Bethlehem to Calvary. "And your soul too a sword shall pierce." Mary is our Spiritual Mother, and the mother always understands her children and consoles them in their troubles. Then, she has that specific mission to love us, received from Jesus on the Cross, to love us only and always, so as to save us! Mary consoles us above all by pointing out the Crucified One and Paradise to us!" (1980)

Therefore, as we honor our Blessed Mother on the Solemnity of the Annunciation and as we draw closer to Holy Week, we honor her as the faithful disciple and exemplar of faith. Let us pray, as we do in the Collect of the Mass on the Feast Day of Our Lady of Sorrows (September 15), "O God, who willed that, when your Son was lifted high on the Cross, his Mother should stand close by and share his suffering, grant that your Church, participating with the Virgin Mary in the Passion of Christ, may merit a share in his Resurrection."

Laetare Sunday

The fourth Sunday of Lent is Laetare Sunday, the Sunday of "rejoic-ing." In Latin, *laetare* means "to rejoice." With the Entrance Anti-phon, we pray, "Rejoice with Jerusalem and be glad because of her, all you who love her; Exult, exult with her, all you who were mourning over her! Oh, that you may suck fully of the milk of her comfort, That you may nurse with delight at her abundant breasts!" (Isaiah 66:10–11). We rejoice because we have reached the midpoint of Lent, and soon we will celebrate Easter.

Even though we are still in the penitential season of Lent, to show our joy, priests may wear rose vestments instead of violet. Altars may be decorated with flowers. Also, instrumental music is permitted.

Nevertheless, this midpoint celebration ought to be seen as a check-up time to ask ourselves: "How well have I kept my Lenten resolutions? Have I prayed daily? Have I been faithful to my sac-rifices? Have I carried the cross by performing the corporal and spiritual works of mercy? Have I made a good examination of conscience and gone to confession? Have I attended the Stations of the Cross?" With the check-up, we resolve once again to continue on with renewed strength so we can celebrate Easter with great joy.

Laetare Sunday was also called "Mothering Sunday." On this day, the faithful remembered their own baptism and would visit their "mother" church, either the church where they had been baptized or the cathedral church. In the Tridentine Mass, the Epistle for this Sunday is from Galatians (4:22–31) and recounts, "We are children not of the slave woman but of the freeborn woman." The Gospel passage is the multiplication of the loaves (Jn 6:1–15). For this reason, the custom arose that children would then return home with flowers, particularly roses, that had been used to decorate the altars to present to their mothers. The families would also enjoy sweet simnel cakes (a fruit cake with layers of almond paste or marzipan) topped with a scallop decoration to remind them of the scallop shell used for pouring water at baptism.

Another interesting point: On Laetare Sunday, the pope will bless and send a golden rose, a sign of spiritual joy, as an honor to a person or institution in recognition of a special service or loyalty. For example, Pope Benedict XVI honored the Basilica of the Immaculate Conception in Washington, D.C. with such a rose.

Fifth Sunday of Lent: Passiontide

Beginning on the Fifth Sunday of Lent, the crosses and sacred images in the Church may be covered in purple. Traditionally, the fifth Sunday of Lent was called Passion Sunday. In the Tridentine Mass, the Gospel recounts our Lord's confrontation with the Pharisees, which concludes, "They picked up stones to throw at him; but Jesus hid and went out of the temple area" (Jn 8:59). For this reason, to remind us of Jesus's hiding, crucifixes and statues have been covered with purple cloth beginning this Sunday. The cross will remain covered until the end of the celebration of the Lord's passion on Good Friday, while sacred images will remain covered until the beginning of the Easter Vigil.

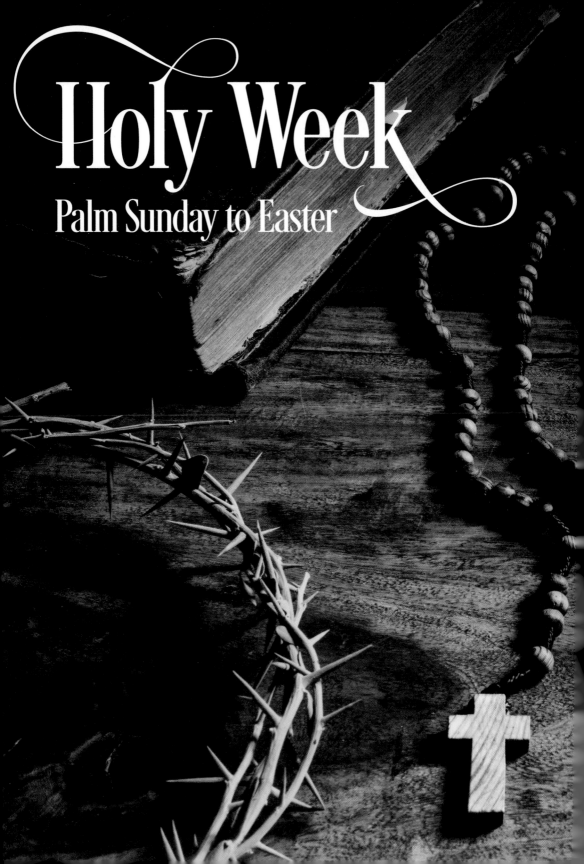

Holy Week

Palm Sunday to Easter

Palm Sunday

Palm Sunday, or Palm Sunday of the Passion of the Lord, begins Holy Week. On this day, we remember how our Lord triumphantly entered Jerusalem as the crowds chanted, "Hosanna to the Son of David; blessed is he who comes in the name of the Lord; hosanna in the highest" (Mt 21:9).

Mass this day begins with a procession—simple or solemn depending upon the parish circumstances—which includes the blessing of the palm branches and a reading of the Gospel account of our Lord's entry into Jerusalem. After the opening greeting, the priest addresses the congregation:

Dear brethren, since the beginning of Lent until now we have prepared our hearts by penance and charitable works. Today we gather together to herald with the whole Church the beginning of the celebration of our Lord's Paschal Mystery, that is to say, of His Passion and Resurrection. For it was to accomplish this mystery that he entered His own city of Jerusalem. Therefore, with all faith and devotion, let us commemorate the Lord's entry into the city for our celebration, following in His footsteps, so that, being made by His grace partakers of the Cross, we may have a share also in His Resurrection and in His life. (Roman Missal)

Having set the stage for the celebration of Holy Week, the priest blesses the palm branches and reads the account of our Lord's entry into Jerusalem. The Holy Mass will then continue with the Collect. For the Gospel reading, the Passion Narrative is proclaimed, which again provides an overview for the celebration of Holy Week.

Why Palms and What to Do With Them

In the ancient world, palms symbolized victory, goodness, strength, and well-being. For this reason, King Solomon, when building the Temple in Jerusalem, had carved figures of cherubim, palm trees, and open flowers on the walls of both the inner and outer rooms. Psalm 92:13 reads, "The just shall flourish like the palm tree."

In Christian iconography, the palm branch represented a martyr's triumph over suffering and persecution. In the catacombs of Rome, frescoes depicting the early martyrs show them holding palm branches, or a palm branch is inscribed on a martyr's tomb next to his or her name. St. John, in the Book of Revelation, described the saints in heaven who died as martyrs: "They stood before the throne and the Lamb, wearing white robes and holding palm branches in their hands" (7:9).

Other traditions surrounding palms include the following: A palm tree sheltered the Holy Family when they rested on their flight into Egypt to escape the wrath of King Herod. St. Michael the Archangel presented the Blessed Virgin Mary a palm branch to announce her approaching passing from this life; in turn, as she fell into her "sleep" (i.e., her dormition). She handed it to St. John, who led the procession of the apostles who carried her body to the tomb in Jerusalem, from which she would be assumed into heavenly glory.

Mindful then that the blessed palm branches represent the victory, goodness, strength, and well-being won by our Lord's saving action and encourage us to remain ever-faithful witnesses, traditionally they are displayed with a crucifix or sacred image. They may also be woven into a cross and displayed. In Eastern European countries, pieces of palm were buried in the gardens, pastures, farmland, and placed in the barns and other buildings for protection against inclement weather and disease. Another Eastern European tradition was to stick a piece of palm in the dough of the bread to be baked for Easter.

FIG SUNDAY

Palm Sunday is also called Fig Sunday, particularly in England. People eat figs or fig pudding to commemorate Jesus's cursing the fig tree the morning after his entry into Jerusalem. We read, "When he was going back to the city in morning, he was hungry. Seeing a fig tree by the road, he went over to it, but found nothing on it except leaves. And he said to it, 'May no fruit ever come from you again'" (Mt 21:18–22).

The fig tree represents both the physical and spiritual health of Israel. During the reign of King Solomon, "Judah and Israel lived in security, every man under his vine or under his fig tree from Dan to Beer-sheba, as long as Solomon lived" (1 Kgs 5:5). God spoke through the Prophet Hosea: "Like grapes in the desert, I found Israel; Like the first fruits of the fig tree in its prime, I considered your fathers" (9:10).

However, when Israel forgot the covenant, broke the

commandments, and sinned, and even turned to false gods, the prophets spoke of how the fig trees were barren and fruitless. For example, Joel prophesied: "The vine has dried up, the fig tree is withered" (1:12). While Habakkuk lamented the condition of Israel, he prophesied hope, "For though the fig tree blossom not nor fruit be on the vines, . . . yet will I rejoice in the LORD and exult in my saving God. GOD, my Lord, is my strength" (3:17–19).

Therefore, our Lord cursed the fig tree because of the sinful condition of Israel and the refusal of the Jewish leaders in particular to accept him as the Messiah. Recall that after the Palm Sunday triumphal entry, our Lord cleansed the Temple of money changers and merchants of animals, calling it a "den of thieves" (Mt 21:13). Nevertheless, through his passion, death, and resurrection, our Lord will free the people of sin, make a new covenant, and establish a new People of God, the Church.

Spy Wednesday

Spy Wednesday is the Wednesday of Holy Week. On Monday, the Gospel passage (Jn 12:1–11) is about Jesus visiting the home of Lazarus, Martha, and Mary Magdalene. Here, Mary used a pound of costly perfume made of aromatic spikenard to anoint the feet of Jesus. Judas Iscariot protested, "Why was this perfume not sold? It could have brought three hundred silver pieces, and the money have been given to the poor?" St. John noted that Judas did not say this because he was concerned for the poor, but because he was a thief and stole from the common purse.

On Tuesday, the Gospel passage (Jn 13:21–33, 36–38) recounts the Last Supper. Here, Jesus announced that one of the apostles would betray him. Although Jesus gave a bit of food to Judas as a sign of friendship, Satan entered that apostle's heart and he went out into the night.

On this day, Spy Wednesday, Judas went to the chief priests and said, "What are you willing to give me if I hand him over to you?" They paid Judas thirty pieces of silver, and he kept looking for— spying—the opportunity to betray our Lord (cf. Mt 26).

Tenebrae

Tenebrae, meaning "darkness" in Latin, is traditionally celebrated during the praying of Matins and Lauds during the Holy Triduum, which begins with the Mass of the Lord's Supper. However, it is now oftentimes celebrated the evening of Spy Wednesday. A special triangular-shaped candelabra which holds fifteen candles is erected. At the beginning of the service, all fifteen candles are lit and the rest of the church is in darkness.

The service is sad and mournful. The service may consist of psalms or selections from the Book of Lamentations. At the end of each one, a candle is extinguished, beginning at the bottom of the candelabra and working back and forth until only the very top candle is lit.

After the final selection, the last candle is extinguished. The church is now in complete darkness. A loud clash sounds, made by the organ or the banging of hymnals on the pews, to symbolize the death of Jesus. This is known as the *strepitus* (in Latin, "loud noise"), and symbolizes the death of Jesus. We read in the Gospel, "And behold, the veil of the sanctuary was torn in two from top to bottom. The earth quaked, rocks were split, tombs were opened" (Mt 27:51–52).

If the parish does not have a Tenebrae service, a version of it can be done as a family. One does not need to have an elaborate candelabra, nor necessarily fifteen candles. For example, a family could have five candles set up and then recite the Five Sorrowful Mysteries of the Rosary. At the end of each decade, one candle would be extinguished so that after the fifth decade, "Jesus dies on the cross," the last candle would be extinguished and the *strepitus* sounded.

A Spiritual Exercise

Spy Wednesday makes us pause and ask ourselves, "What price do I put on Jesus? Have I 'sold him' for something I value more?" These questions make a person uncomfortable, but when we neglect to pray but have time for computer games, or skip Mass because of vacation or social events, are we not selling Jesus for something we value more? Therefore, we can use this day for a final examination of conscience and a review of our Lenten preparation. If a good confession has not been made or now ought to be made, the time has come to do so before we enter into the Holy Triduum and celebrate Easter.

Another exercise is to ponder the prayer in the Divine Liturgy of the Byzantine Church, which the congregation prays before receiving Holy Communion:

O Lord, I believe and profess that you are truly Christ, the Son of the Living God, who came into the world to save sinners of whom I am the first.

Accept me today as a partaker of your mystical supper, O Son of God, for I will not reveal your mystery to your enemies, nor will I give you a kiss as did Judas, but like the thief I profess you:

> Remember me, O Lord, when you come into your kingdom.
>
> Remember me, O Master, when you come into your kingdom.
>
> Remember me, O holy One, when you come into your kingdom.
>
> May the partaking of your holy mysteries, O Lord, be not for my judgment or condemnation, but for the healing of soul and body.
>
> O Lord, I also believe and profess that this, which I am about to receive, is truly your most precious body and your life-giving blood, which, I pray, make me worthy to receive for the remission of all my sins and for life everlasting. Amen.
>
> O God, be merciful to me, a sinner.
>
> O God, cleanse me of my sins and have mercy on me.
>
> O Lord, forgive me for I have sinned without number.

Holy Thursday Morning: The Chrism Mass

On Holy Thursday morning, the bishop celebrates the Chrism Mass at the cathedral, traditionally the only Mass celebrated in the diocese that morning. (In some dioceses that encompass a large territory, the Chrism Mass may be celebrated on another day of Holy Week so that the clergy and the people may attend.) This tradition is rooted in the early Church, as noted in the *Gelasian Sacramentary* (named after Pope Gelasius I, d. 496).

As the Roman Missal states, "This Mass, which the Bishop concelebrates with his presbyterate, should be, as it were, a manifestation of the Priests' communion with their Bishop." Priests renew their sacred promises. The bishop asks his priests the following three questions, to which the priests respond, "I am":

Beloved son, on the anniversary of that day when Christ our Lord conferred his priesthood on his Apostles and on us, are you

resolved to renew, in the presence of your Bishop and God's Holy people, the promises you once made?

Are you resolved to be more united with the Lord Jesus and more closely conformed to Him, denying yourselves and confirming those promises about sacred duties towards Christ's Church which, prompted by love of Him, you willingly and joyfully pledged on the day of your priestly ordination?

Are you resolved to be faithful stewards of the mysteries of God in the Holy Eucharist and the other liturgical rites and to discharge faithfully the sacred office of teaching, following Christ the Head and Shepherd, not seeking any gain, but moved only by zeal for souls?

After these questions, the bishop exhorts the congregation to pray for the priests who serve the diocese and for himself, to which they respond, "Christ, hear us. Christ, graciously hear us":

As for you, dearest sons and daughters, pray for your Priests, that the Lord may pour out His gifts abundantly upon them, and keep them faithful as ministers of Christ, the High Priest, so that they may lead you to Him, who is the source of salvation.

And pray also for me, that I may be faithful to the apostolic office entrusted to me in my lowliness and that in your midst I may be made day after day a living and more perfect image of Christ, the Priest, the Good Shepherd, the Teacher and the Servant of all.

After this renewal of priestly promises and the exhortation of the faithful, the bishop proceeds with the blessing of the holy oils which will be used for the sacraments: the Oil of Catechumens for Baptism (*Oleum Catechumenorum* or *Oleum Sanctorum*), the Oil of the Infirm for Anointing of the Sick (*Oleum Infirmorum*), and the Sacred Chrism for Baptism, Confirmation, and Holy Orders (*Sacrum Chrisma*). After the Mass, each pastor (or designate) fills the parish's oil stocks with the newly blessed oils for use in the parish during the year.

A spiritual exercise would be to find our sacramental records (if you don't have them, they may be found at the churches where you received each sacrament) and reflect on the great graces we have received through these sacraments. Also, we should pray for the bishop and priests of our particular diocese and parish that they may be courageous witnesses of the faith and preach the Gospel with courage and conviction. Despite the recent travails and revelations, as faithful Catholics who know that Christ founded his Church to help us on the way to heaven, we must always remember that we need holy bishops and priests and should pray for them. Pope St. John Paul II, in his first Holy Thursday Letter to Priests (1979), reflected:

Dear brothers, you who have borne "the burden of the day and the heat," who have put your hand to the plough and do not turn back, and perhaps even more those of you who are doubtful of the meaning of your vocation or of the value of your service; think of the places where people anxiously await a priest, and where for many years, feeling the lack of such a priest, they do not cease to hope for his presence. And sometimes it happens that they meet in an abandoned shrine, and place on the altar a stole which they still keep, and recite all the prayers of the Eucharistic Liturgy; and then at the moment that corresponds to the transubstantiation a deep silence comes down upon them, a silence sometimes broken by a sob . . . [sic] so ardently do they desire to hear the words that only the lips of a priest can efficaciously utter. So much do they desire Eucharistic Communion, in which they can share only through the ministry of a priest, just as they also so eagerly wait to hear the divine words of pardon: *Ego te absolvo a peccatis tuis*! So deeply do they feel the absence of a priest among them! . . . Such places are not lacking in the world. So if one of you doubts the meaning of his priesthood, if he thinks it is "socially" fruitless or useless, reflect on this!

Yes, this day pray for your bishops and priests! Pray also for seminarians preparing for the priesthood, and for young men to heed Christ's call to serve as a priest. How easily for us to forget or take for granted those who have generously served the Lord and the Church as priests! This day, we must renew our faith and commit ourselves to serve the Lord wholeheartedly so that we can create "a pleasing odor" in the world in which we live though our words and deeds.

The Holy Oils

Throughout the Bible, various references indicate the importance of olive oil in daily life. Oil was used in cooking, particularly in the making of bread, that basic food substance for nourishment (see Nm 11:7–9), as a fuel for lamps (see Mt 25:1–9), and as a healing agent in medicine (see Is 1:6; Lk 10:34). Moreover, the Jews anointed the head of a guest with oil as a sign of welcome (see Lk 7:46), used it to beautify one's appearance (see Ru 3:3), and to prepare a body for burial (see Mk 16:1). In religious practices, the Jews also used oil to offer sacrifices (see Ex 29:40), to dedicate a memorial stone in honor of God (see Gn 28:18), and to consecrate the meeting tent, the ark of the covenant, the table, the lampstand, the laver, the altar of incense, and the altar of holocausts (see Ex 31:26–29). The use of oil was clearly a part of the daily life of the people.

Sacred Scripture also attests to the spiritual symbolism of oil. For instance, Psalm 23:5 reads, "You anoint my head with oil," signifying favor and strength from the Lord; and Psalm 45:8 reads, "You love justice and hate wrongdoing; therefore God, your God, has anointed you with the oil of gladness above your fellow kings," signifying the special designation from God and the joy of being his servant. Moreover, to be "the anointed" of the Lord indicated receiving a special vocation from him and the empowerment with the Holy Spirit to fulfill that vocation: Jesus, echoing the words of Isaiah, spoke, "The Spirit of the Lord is upon me, because he has anointed me" (Lk 4:18). St. Paul emphasized this point, "The one who gives us security with you in Christ and who anointed us is God" (2 Cor 1:21). Therefore, the symbolism of oil is rich—sanctification, healing, strengthening, beautification, dedication, consecration, and sacrifice.

Given this heritage, the early Church adopted the use of olive oil for its sacramental rituals. The Oil of Catechumens is used with the sacrament of Baptism. St. Hippolytus, in his *Apostolic Tradition* (AD 215), wrote of an "Oil of Exorcism" used to anoint the candidates immediately before baptism. This practice still continues: In the current baptismal liturgy, the priest offers the prayer of exorcism and then anoints with the Oil of Catechumens the person to be baptized on the chest, saying, "We anoint you with the oil of salvation in the name of Christ our Savior; may He strengthen you with His power, who lives and reigns forever and ever." Anointing with the Oil of Catechumens following a prayer of exorcism may also take place during the period of the Catechumentate on one or several occasions. In both cases this anointing symbolizes the person's need for the help and strength of God to sever the bondage of the past and to overcome the opposition of the devil so that he may profess his faith, come to baptism, and live as a child of God.

The Oil of the Infirm is used in the sacrament of the Anointing of the Sick (formerly known as Extreme Unction). St. James wrote, "Is anyone among you sick? He should summon the presbyters of the church, and they should pray over him and anoint [him] with oil in the name of the Lord, and the prayer of faith will save the sick person, and the Lord will raise him up. If he has committed any sins, he will be forgiven" (Jas 5:14–15).

The *Apostolic Tradition* of St. Hippolytus recorded one of the earliest formulas for blessing the Oil of the Infirm. Also, in the early Church, a priest (or several priests) would bless this oil at the time it was to be used, a tradition that has been retained in the Eastern Churches. However, in the Latin Rite, at least since the time of the Middles Ages, priests have used oil blessed by the bishop; for instance, St. Boniface in 730 ordered all priests in Germany to use the Oil of the Infirm blessed by bishops only. Presently, the priest, anointing the forehead of the person, says, "Through this holy anointing, may the Lord in His love and mercy help you with the grace of the Holy Spirit," and then anointing the hands, says, "May the Lord who frees you from sin, save you and raise you up." Another body part may also be anointed if the hands are not accessible or if there is another particular need.

Finally, Holy Chrism is a mixture of olive oil and balsam, an aromatic resin. This oil is linked with the sanctification of individuals. In the Old Testament times, the priest, prophets, and kings of the Jewish people were anointed with chrism. This oil is used in the sacraments of Baptism, Confirmation, and Holy Orders since they impart an indelible sacramental character.

The blessing of the Holy Chrism is different from that of the other oils: Here the bishop breathes over the vessel of chrism, a gesture which symbolizes both the Holy Spirit coming down to consecrate this oil and the life-giving, sanctifying nature of the "indelible character" sacraments for which it is used. Recall how our Lord "breathed" on the apostles on the night of Easter, saying, 'Receive the Holy Spirit'" (Jn 20:22). The concelebrants at the Chrism Mass also extend their right hands toward the chrism as the bishop says the consecratory prayer, signifying that in union with their bishop they share "in the authority by which Christ Himself builds up and sanctifies and rules His Body," the Church (Vatican II, *Decree on the Ministry and Life of Priests*, no. 2).

Regarding baptism, St. Hippolytus in the *Apostolic Tradition* spoke of an anointing after the actual baptism with the "oil of thanksgiving." Similarly, right after the actual baptism in the present rite, the priest anoints the person on the crown of the head with chrism, saying, "God the Father of our Lord Jesus Christ has freed you from sin and given you a new birth by water and the Holy

Spirit. He now anoints you with the chrism of salvation. As Christ was anointed Priest, Prophet, and King, so may you live always as a member of His body, sharing everlasting life. Amen."

In the sacrament of Confirmation, the bishop anoints the forehead of the candidate with Holy Chrism saying, "Be sealed with the gift of the Holy Spirit."

Holy Chrism is also used in the sacrament of Holy Orders. In the ordination rite of a priest, the bishop anoints with chrism the palms of each new priest. In the ordination rite of a bishop, the consecrating bishop anoints the head of the new bishop.

Finally, Holy Chrism is used in the dedication ceremony of a church. Here the bishop anoints the altar, pouring Holy Chrism on the middle of the altar and on each of its four corners. It is recommended that the bishop anoint the entire altar. After anointing the altar, he anoints the walls of the Church in twelve or four places that are marked by crosses.

As we prepare to celebrate the Holy Triduum, each of us should pause and reflect on the sacraments we have received, particularly those character sacraments of Baptism, Confirmation, and, if one is a deacon or priest, Holy Orders, and give thanks to God.

Holy Chrism is a particularly apt symbol to remind us of this sacred seal. Just as an oil stain is permanent on clothing, so the anointing with Holy Chrism signifies the permanent mark on our soul. Also, being a perfumed oil, it reminds us that we are called to "smell" differently in this world; that is, as Christians, we should be recognizably distinct from pagans—our lives should reflect our faith. Here we are reminded of what the Lord said to the House of Israel: "As a pleasing odor I will accept you, when I have brought you from among the nations and gathered you out of the countries over which you were scattered; and by means of you I will manifest my holiness in the sight of the nations" (Ez 20:41).

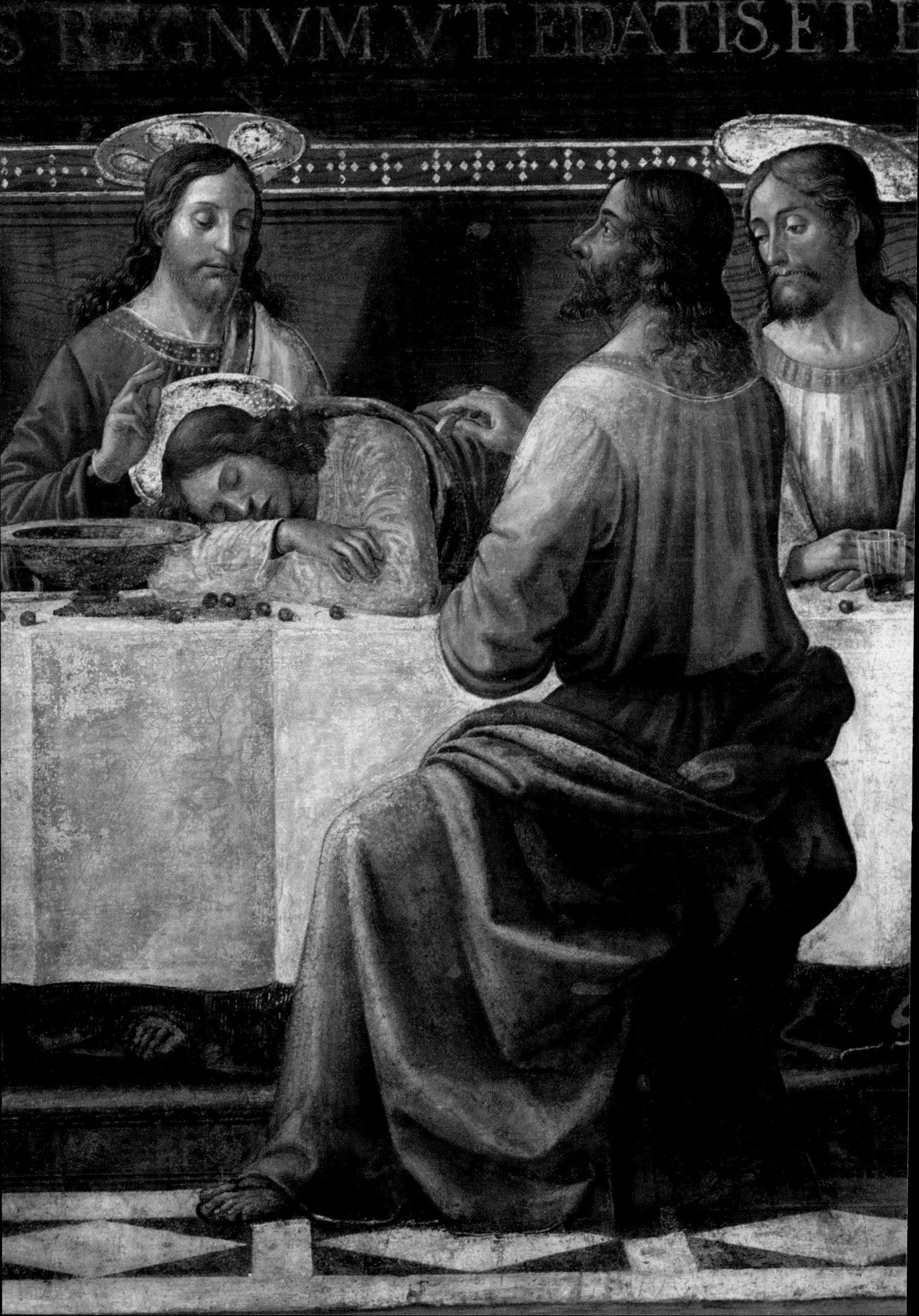
REGNVM,VT EDATIS,ET

Holy Thursday: Mass of the Lord's Supper

Holy Thursday evening begins the Sacred Triduum with the Mass of the Lord's Supper. The Holy Triduum ought to be seen as "one big Mass," which begins with the Mass of the Lord's Supper, continues through the Liturgy of the Passion on Good Friday, and concludes with the Easter Vigil. For this reason, there is no final blessing until the Easter Vigil.

On Holy Thursday evening, the faithful remember the Last Supper when our Lord instituted the Holy Eucharist and the holy priesthood. Sometimes this day is called Maundy Thursday, recalling Jesus's mandate to the apostles: "I give you a new commandment [in Latin, *mandatum*]: love one another" (Jn 13:34). Our Lord washed the feet of his apostles (see Jn 13:1–11) to show them that as he had come to serve, so must they; therefore, after the homily, the priest washes the feet of twelve of the faithful (traditionally, men to represent the apostles).

An interesting liturgical point is that the sanctuary bells are rung during the singing of the Gloria. They then remain silent until the singing of the Gloria during the Easter Vigil Mass. Therefore, at the elevation of the Sacred Host and Chalice after the consecration, a "clapper" is used instead of bells; that is, a wooden instrument that makes a knocking noise.

Following the Prayer after Communion and then omitting the final blessing, the Most Blessed Sacrament is transferred in procession to a repository, preferably outside of the church. Here the faithful may remain and adore in prayerful silence for three hours until midnight. This devotion reminds the faithful of the time our Lord spent in the Garden of Gethsemane, praying and preparing for his imminent sacrifice.

Another tradition is to visit three different parishes and pray at the altar of repose. This practice reminds the faithful that during his three hours of prayer, Jesus found his apostles asleep and had to awaken them (see Mt 26:36–46). We heed our Lord's words, "Watch and pray that you may not undergo the test. The spirit is willing, but the flesh is weak" (Mt 26:41). This night, we must stay awake and be with Jesus.

Finally, after Mass, the altar is stripped of its linens and candles. The tabernacle remains empty and the door open. The darkness of Good Friday has begun.

Passover on Thursday or Passover on Friday?

In the Gospels, there seems to be confusion over the celebration of Passover: At the Last Supper, Jesus celebrated the Passover meal with his apostles on Holy Thursday. However, the Gospel of St. John indicates that the bodies of Jesus and the thieves had to be taken down from the cross before Passover began on Good Friday evening. So what is the answer?

In addressing this question, let's begin with a simple overview of the chronology of events presented in the Synoptic Gospels; that is, Matthew, Mark, and Luke. First, Jesus spoke of celebrating the Passover feast with his apostles: "On the first day of the Feast of Unleavened Bread, the disciples approached Jesus and said, 'Where do you want us to prepare for you to eat the Passover?' He said, 'Go into the city to a certain man and tell him, "The teacher says, 'My appointed time draws near; in your house I shall celebrate the Passover with my disciples'"'" (Mt 26:17–19). (A similar record is found in St. Mark and St. Luke.) Keep in mind that on the first day of the Feast of Unleavened Bread, the lambs would have been slaughtered in the Temple and readied for the Passover meal after sunset (about 6:00 p.m.).

Second, that night, after supper, Jesus would have prayed in the Garden of Gethsemane and then been arrested. On Friday morning, "as soon as morning came" (Mk 15:1), the chief priests, elders, and scribes took Jesus to Pilate (about 6:00 a.m.). Arriving at Calvary, the soldiers crucified Jesus at 9:00 a.m. (see Mk 15:25). About midday (12:00 noon), darkness covered the whole land until midafternoon (3:00 p.m.), at which time, Jesus died.

Third, after Jesus's death, Joseph of Arimathea asked Pilate for his body for burial. The body had to be buried before sunset, "since it was the day of preparation, the day before the sabbath" (Mk 15:42). Following the synoptics, it *appears* that the Jews as well as Jesus and the apostles celebrated the Passover meal on Thursday, and then Jesus was crucified on Friday.

However, the Gospel of John highlighted that the Jews would be celebrating the Passover meal the night of Good Friday: When the chief priest, elders, and scribes brought Jesus to Pilate on Friday morning, "they themselves did not enter the praetorium, in order not to be defiled so that they could eat the Passover" (Jn 18:28) that Friday evening. So, how do we reconcile the Gospel accounts? Are there some overlooked details that help clarify the matter?

First, Passover was celebrated on the fifteenth day of the month of Nisan. Remember, for the Jews, the new day begins at sunset, so the lambs would have been slaughtered on the afternoon of Nisan 14, and then after sunset on Nisan 15, the Passover meal would have been shared. Presuming Jesus died in the year AD 33, the Passover meal would have been a Friday evening celebration (which would also coincide with the beginning of the Sabbath). Because of changes in how the Jews calculated their dates, scholars posit that whether the actual date was AD 33 or three years earlier would not matter.

Second, Pope Benedict XVI, in his *Jesus of Nazareth Vol. 3*, noted that having a trial and crucifixion take place on the day of Passover (Friday) is problematic (with the Passover meal eaten the preceding Thursday evening). He highlighted, as recorded in

Mark, that while the chief priests, elders, and scribes looked for the opportunity to arrest and kill Jesus, they decided, "Not during the festival [Passover], for fear that there may be a riot among the people" (Mk 14:2), meaning that they would have wanted to avoid any turmoil after sunset on Thursday. Therefore, it makes more sense that Friday evening would have marked the beginning of Passover; that is, after the crucifixion.

Third, in the Gospel of Mark, when Jesus instructed his apostles about preparing for the Passover, he said, "Go into the city and a man will meet you, carrying a jar of water. Follow him" (Mk 14:13). Some Scripture scholars note that only women carried water jars. However, among the Essenes, a conservative and separatist group from the dominant Pharisee-Sadducee establishment, men did carry large water jars for their ritual ablutions with water. The Essenes also followed a different calendar, again posing the possibility of an earlier Passover celebration.

So now we can draw a quick summary: Jesus had the Last Supper on Holy Thursday, a Passover meal—his Passover meal. On Good Friday, he was condemned by Pilate and crucified. At 3:00 p.m., Jesus died. During this time, the lambs were being slaughtered in the Temple, preparing for the official Passover meal which took place that evening after sunset; Jesus, the High Priest, is offering himself as the Lamb of God, now being sacrificed on the altar of the cross. He is then buried before sunset.

Therefore, Jesus celebrated a Passover—his *own*, new Passover—on Holy Thursday evening, not the Passover of the old covenant celebrated on Friday evening. In the Passover of the old covenant, a one-year-old, unblemished, male lamb was sacrificed, roasted, and eaten with unleavened bread. Note that the Gospels made no mention of procuring or sharing a Passover lamb (which would not have been available until Friday afternoon, when he is

crucified). However, Jesus, sinless, is the new Passover Lamb. Even his bones were not broken on the cross (see Jn 19:33). By his blood, the new and everlasting covenant is made. By his sacrifice, a new Exodus takes place—freedom from the slavery of sin, and the hope of entry into the promised land of heaven. Unlike the Passover lamb that was sacrificed and eaten, Jesus rose from the dead. While the Passover of the old covenant was eaten among family members with the father presiding, the new Passover is eaten among the members of the Church with the Lord presiding. And, while the Passover of the old covenant focused on the flesh and blood of the lamb and the Exodus event, the new Passover is a sharing the Body and Blood of the Lord Jesus himself, and he commanded us, "Do this in remembrance of me."

Another interesting point: The Passover of the old covenant involved the sharing of four cups of wine. The first, the *kiddush* cup, or the cup of sanctification; the second, the *haggadah* cup, or the cup of proclamation at which time the father recounts the Exodus event; the third, the *berakah* cup, or blessing cup, drunk after the meal was finished; and the fourth, the *zebah todah* cup, or the cup of thanksgiving at which time the Hallel Psalms (113–118) were sung.

Consider the Last Supper as recorded in the Gospels: "And likewise the cup after they had eaten, saying, 'This cup is the new covenant in my blood, which will be shed for you'" (Lk 22:20), indicating the *berakah* cup. And then, "when they had sung a hymn" (Mt 26:30) referring to the Hallel Psalms, Jesus and the apostles went out to the Garden of Gethsemane, where our Lord prayed, "Father, if you are willing, take this cup away from me; still, not my will but yours be done" (Lk 22:42). The fourth and final cup of Jesus's Passover was drunk on the cross: "When Jesus had taken the wine, he said, 'It is finished.' And bowing his head, he handed over the spirit" (Jn 19:30).

Pope Benedict wrote,

> One thing emerges clearly from the entire tradition: essentially, this farewell meal was not the old Passover, but the new one, which Jesus accomplished in this context. Even though the meal that Jesus shared with the Twelve was not a Passover meal according to the ritual prescriptions of Judaism, nevertheless, in retrospect, the inner connection of the whole event with Jesus' death and Resurrection stood out clearly. It was Jesus' Passover. And in this sense he both did and did not celebrate the Passover: the old rituals could not be carried out—when their time came, Jesus had already died. But he had given Himself, and thus he had truly celebrated the Passover with them. The old was not abolished; it was simply brought to its full meaning." (*Jesus of Nazareth* Vol. 3, p. 114)

And how beautiful it is to know that Jesus's Passover continues in our Holy Mass!

The Gift of the Holy Eucharist

As Catholics, we firmly believe that the real presence of Christ is in the Holy Eucharist. The Second Vatican Council's *Decree on the Ministry and Life of Priests* asserts:

> The other sacraments, as well as with every ministry of the Church and every work of the apostolate, are tied together with the Eucharist and are directed toward it. The Most Blessed Eucharist contains the entire spiritual boon of the Church, that is, Christ himself, our Pasch and Living Bread, by the action of the Holy Spirit through his very flesh vital and vitalizing, giving life to men who are thus invited and encouraged to offer themselves, their labors and all created things, together with him. In this light, the Eucharist shows itself as the source and the apex of the whole work of preaching the Gospel." (*Presbyterorum Ordinis*, no. 5)

Our belief in the Holy Eucharist is rooted in Christ himself. Recall the beautiful words of our Lord in the Bread of Life Discourse in the Gospel of John:

> I am the living bread that came down from heaven; whoever eats this bread will live forever; and the bread that I will give is my flesh for the life of the world. . . . Amen, amen, I say to you, unless you eat the flesh of the Son of Man and drink his blood, you do not have life within you. Whoever eats my flesh and drinks my blood has eternal life, and I will raise him on the last day. For my flesh is true food, and my blood is true drink. Whoever eats my flesh and drinks my blood remains in me and I in him. Just as the living Father sent me and I have life because of the Father, so also the one who feeds on me will have life because of me. (Jn 6:51, 53–57)

Note that none of this language is symbolic or poetic—Jesus meant what he said. Moreover, even when there was grumbling and objections, and even after some disciples abandoned our Lord because of this teaching, Jesus nowhere said, "Oh please, stop. Come back. You misunderstood me. I really meant this symbolically. I'll change my teaching." Our Lord stood by his teaching.

The meaning of the Bread of Life Discourse becomes clearer at the Last Supper on the first Holy Thursday. There Jesus gathered his apostles to share what was literally his last supper. According to the Gospel of Matthew, Jesus took unleavened bread and wine—two sources of basic nourishment. He took the bread, blessed it, gave thanks, broke it, and gave it to the apostles, saying, "Take this and eat it; this is my body." He took the cup of wine, gave thanks, gave it to his apostles, and said, "All of you must drink from it for this is my blood, the blood of the covenant, to be poured out on behalf of many for the forgiveness of sins." If we extracted the words of consecration recorded in the Last Supper accounts of the Gospels and distilled them, we would have the words of consecration used at Mass (see Mt 26:26–30; Mk 14:22–26; Lk 22:14–20).

Think of those words! Jesus was not just giving to the apostles blessed bread and wine. He was giving his whole life—Body, Blood, Soul, and Divinity. He was giving his very self. How true that was! The next day, Jesus's body hung upon the altar of the cross. His blood was spilled to wash away our sins. As priest, he offered the perfect sacrifice for the remission of sin. However, this sacrifice was not death-rendering but life-giving; for three days later, our Lord rose from the dead conquering both sin and death. Yes, the perfect, everlasting covenant of life and love with God was made by our Lord Jesus Christ.

This whole mystery is preserved in the Most Holy Eucharist and the Sacrifice of the Mass. We too take unleavened bread and wine, two sources of nourishment. By the will of the Father, the work of the Holy Spirit, and priesthood of Jesus entrusted to his ordained priests, and through the words of consecration, that bread and wine is transformed into the Body, Blood, Soul and Divinity of Jesus. Yes, the bread and wine do not change in characteristics (or technically, the accidents); they still look the same, taste and smell the same, and hold the same shape. However, the reality, "the what it is," the substance, does change. We do not receive bread and wine; we receive the Body and Blood of Christ. We call this change of substance *transubstantiation*, a term used at the Fourth Lateran Council (1215) and asserted again by our Pope St. John Paul II in *Ecclesia de Eucharistia* (no. 15). Therefore, each time we celebrate

Mass, we are plunged into the whole ever-present, everlasting mystery of Holy Thursday, Good Friday, Easter, and the Ascension. We share intimately in the life of our Lord through Holy Eucharist.

In *Ecclesia de Eucharistia*, Pope St. John Paul II highlighted these very points: "At every celebration of the Eucharist, we are spiritually brought back to the paschal Triduum: to the events of the evening of Holy Thursday, to the Last Supper, and to what followed it. The institution of the Eucharist sacramentally anticipated the events which were about to take place, beginning with the agony in Gethsemane" (no. 3). Moreover, in and through the Holy Eucharist, Pope St. John Paul II taught that we can contemplate the face of Christ because he is truly present:

> To contemplate Christ involves being able to recognize him wherever he manifests himself, in his many forms of presence, but above all in the living sacrament of his Body and Blood. *The Church draws her life from Christ in the Eucharist*; by him she is fed and by him she is enlightened. The Eucharist is both a mystery of faith and a "mystery of light." Whenever the Church celebrates the Eucharist, the faithful can in some way relive the experience of the two disciples on the road to Emmaus: "their eyes were opened and they recognized him." (no. 6)

Since the days of the first apostles, the Catholic Church has always cherished this treasure. St. Paul wrote:

> I received from the Lord what I also handed on to you, that the Lord Jesus, on the night he was handed over, took bread, and, after he had given thanks, broke it and said, "This is my body that is for you. Do this in remembrance of me." In the same way also the cup, after supper, saying, "This cup is the new covenant

in my blood. Do this, as often as you drink it, in remembrance of me." For as often as you eat this bread and drink the cup, you proclaim the death of the Lord until he comes." (1 Cor 11:23–26)

During the days of Roman persecution, to clearly distinguish the Eucharist from the cultic rite of Mithra and to dispel Roman charges of cannibalism, St. Justin Martyr (d. 165) wrote in his *First Apology*, "We do not consume the Eucharistic bread and wine as if it were ordinary food and drink, for we have been taught that as Jesus Christ our Savior became a man of flesh and blood by the power of the Word of God, so also the food that our flesh and blood assimilate of its nourishment becomes the flesh and blood of the incarnate Jesus by the power of His own words contained in the prayer of thanksgiving."

Later, the Council of Trent in 1551 addressed the heretical views of the Reformers. Remember, Zwingli and Calvin believed that Christ was present only "in sign"; Luther believed in consubstantiation whereby the Eucharist is both body and blood and bread and wine; and Melancthon believed that the Eucharist reverts back to just bread and wine after communion.

Trent's *Decree on the Most Holy Eucharist* specified, "In the Blessed Sacrament of the Holy Eucharist, after the consecration of the bread and wine, our Lord Jesus Christ, true God and man, is truly, really, and substantially contained under the appearances of those perceptible realities. For there is no contradiction in the fact that our Savior always sits at the right hand of the Father in Heaven according to His natural way of existing and that, nevertheless, in His substance he is sacramentally present to us in many other places." Therefore, no faithful, knowledgeable Catholic would say that the Holy Eucharist is just bread and wine or even just symbolizes the Body and Blood of Christ. Yes, we pray for

grace that we may believe more strongly each day in this precious gift of Christ himself. Perhaps we should dwell on the words of St. Thomas Aquinas in *Adoro Te Devote*:

> Humbly we adore thee, Christ, Redeemer King;
> Thou art Lord of heaven, thou to whom we sing.
> God, the Mighty, thou hast come, bearing gifts of grace;
> Son of Adam still thou art, Savior to our race.

> Jesus, Lord, we thank thee for this wondrous bread;
> In our land thou dwellest, by thee we are fed.
> We who share this mystery in thee are made one;
> Every act we offer thee in thy name is done.

> Thou who died to save us livest as our light;
> Though our eyes are blinded, yet our faith gives sight.
> Christ, do thou be merciful, Lamb for sinners slain,
> We in grief confess our guilt; cleanse our souls of stain.

Christ, our God and brother, hear our humble plea,
By this holy banquet keep us joined to thee.
Make us one in loving thee, one in mind and heart,
Till in heaven we are thine, nevermore to part.

Hail, thou Word Incarnate, born from Mary's womb;
Hail, thou Strength immortal, risen from the tomb.
Share with us thy victory, Savior ever blest:
Live more fully in our hearts; be our constant guest.

Faith alone reveals here bread of Paradise:
Faith alone may witness Jesus' sacrifice.
Therefore, Lord, as once of old Thomas gained his sight,
Now increase our feeble faith; shed thy healing light.

Christ, at his last supper, breaking bread, decreed:
"This is my Body, take and eat": heav'nly food indeed!
The he blessed the cup of wine; 'take ye this," he said:
"Drink the chalice of my Blood, soon for sinners shed."

Now with glad thanksgiving, praise Christ glorified;
He in us is present; we in him abide.
Members of his body, we in him are one;
Hail this sacred union, heav'n on earth begun!

A Eucharistic Miracle

To help the faithful believe in the Real Presence of the Holy Eucharist, our Lord has performed Eucharistic miracles over the centuries. The miracle of Lanciano is the first recorded, and many believe the greatest, Eucharistic miracle of the Catholic Church. Keep in mind that, strictly speaking, a miracle is an extraordinary event produced directly by God or by his will and command through an agent, such as a saint. The miracle occurs in a religious context and is a clear sign of supernatural, divine intervention. Most importantly, the miracle arouses within the spectator or recipient a greater conviction of faith in God.

With this in mind, we now turn to a miracle which occurred in the 700s in the town of Lanciano, then known as Anxanum, an ancient Roman city, located southeast of Rome, near the Adriatic Sea. There the monks of St. Basil had established a monastery under the patronage of St. Longinus, traditionally believed to be the centurion at the crucifixion who proclaimed, "Truly, this was the Son of God" (Mt 27:54) and pierced the side of our Lord with his lance (see Jn 19:34).

One day, a certain monk was offering the Holy Sacrifice of the Mass. Although we do not know his identity, an ancient document described him as "versed in the sciences of the world but ignorant in that of God." Apparently, he had been plagued by doubts about transubstantiation: he agonized over whether the bread and wine changed substantially into the Body and Blood of our Lord at the words of consecration and whether our Lord was truly present in the Holy Eucharist.

This time, when the monk pronounced the words of consecration, the host was miraculously changed into flesh and the wine into blood. The monk was awestruck. Weeping joyously, he regained his composure. He called the congregation around the altar and said, "O fortunate witnesses, to whom the Blessed God, to confound my unbelief, has wished to reveal Himself visible to our eyes! Come, brethren, and marvel at our God, so close to us. Behold the Flesh and Blood of our Most Beloved Christ." Those who witnessed the miracle soon spread the news throughout the surrounding area.

Shortly after the occurrence, the Blood coagulated into five globules of different sizes, but the Flesh remained the same. The archbishop ordered an investigation. The testimony of witnesses was recorded. The Flesh and Blood appeared to be human flesh and blood. The archbishop sent a scale for the weighing of the globules: each individual globule weighed the same as the other individual ones (although different in size) or as all five together or as any other combination. Eventually, the Flesh and the globules of Blood were placed in a special ivory reliquary, but not hermetically sealed. Church authorities certified the miracle, although the original document was lost some time in the sixteenth century.

Over the centuries, different religious orders have had custody of the church and the relics: originally the Basilians until 1176, followed by the Benedictines until 1252, and since then by the Franciscans. In 1258, the Franciscans built a new church under the patronage of St. Francis of Assisi to replace the decaying church of St. Longinus. The relics to this day remain at this basilica under the care of the Franciscans.

Since the first basic investigation, the Church has permitted other studies on the relics. In 1574, Monsignor Rodrigues once again weighed the five globules in the presence of witnesses and arrived at the same conclusion. Remember though that eight centuries had passed and no visible sign of deterioration had taken place.

In 1713, the original ivory reliquary was replaced by one of silver and crystal. The Flesh is displayed in a monstrance just like the Sacred Host, and the globules of Blood are in a crystal chalice, which some believe is the actual chalice used by the monk for Mass.

The most thorough study occurred in 1970–1971. Pope St. Paul VI permitted a series of scientific studies on the precious relics

to verify their nature. Dr. Odoardo Linoli, Professor of Anatomy and Pathological Histology and of Chemistry and Clinical Microscopy and head physician of the hospital of Arezzo, conducted the study. He was assisted by Dr. Ruggero Bertelli, Professor Emeritus of Human Anatomy at the University of Siena. The analyses were performed in accord with scientific standards and documented, and Dr. Bertelli independently corroborated Dr. Linoli's findings. In 1981, using more advanced medical technology, Dr. Linoli conducted a second histological study; he not only confirmed the findings but also gathered new information.

The major findings from this research include the following: The Flesh, yellow-brown in color, has the structure of the myocardium (heart wall) and the endocardium, the membrane of fibrous-elastic tissue lining all the cardiac cavities. These have the same appearance as in the human heart. No traces of preservatives were found in the elements.

The blood was also of human origin with the type AB. Proteins in the clotted Blood were normally fractioned with the same percentage ratio as those found in the sero-proteic make-up of normal, fresh human blood. The Blood contained these minerals: chlorides, phosphorus, magnesium, potassium, sodium, and calcium.

Professor Linoli asserted that the blood, if taken from a cadaver, would have deteriorated rapidly. Given that these samples were centuries old, free of preservatives, and never hermetically sealed in the reliquaries, they should have deteriorated. However, he underscored that the samples had the same properties as fresh human blood and flesh.

Moreover, the doctors both concluded that only the skill of a trained pathologist could have obtained such a sample, a tangential cut of the heart—a round cut, thick on the outer edges and lessening gradually and uniformly to the central area.

The beauty of the miracle of Lanciano reflects the words our Lord spoke, "I am the bread of life. . . . Whoever eats my flesh and drinks my blood has eternal life, and I will raise him on the last day. For my flesh is true food, and my blood is true drink. Whoever eats my flesh and drinks my blood remains in me and I in him"

(Jn 6:35, 54–56). We must, therefore, never forget that when we worship at Mass, we witness a miracle, and through the reception of Holy Communion, we share in the divine life of our Savior, his Body, Blood, Soul and Divinity.

Good Friday: Friday of the Passion of the Lord

On Good Friday, the Church celebrates the Liturgy of the Passion of the Lord. No Mass is offered this day. The liturgy begins in silence. After processing and prostrating before the altar, the priest offers the prayer, omitting the normal sign of the cross and greeting. The Liturgy of the Passion consists of three parts: the Liturgy of the Word, which includes the proclamation of the Passion of the Gospel of St. John and the Solemn Intercessions; the Adoration of the Holy Cross follows; and finally Holy Communion from the Holy Eucharist consecrated at the Mass of the Lord's Supper on Holy Thursday evening. The liturgy concludes with the final prayer and blessing (but omitting the sign of the cross). The priest then leaves in silence.

The Liturgy of the Passion is celebrated at 3:00 p.m. to commemorate the hour when Jesus died on the cross. For pastoral reasons, it may be celebrated at another time. Traditionally, the faithful will also pray the Sorrowful Mysteries of the Rosary and the Stations of the Cross on this day. Some parishes also offer meditations on the Seven Last Words—the seven statements our Lord made from the cross. In all, this is a day for quiet reflection, fasting, and abstinence.

What Do We Mean By "the Passion" of Our Lord?

The Passion of Christ, from the Latin *patior*, meaning "suffer," refers to those sufferings our Lord endured for our redemption from the agony in the garden until his death on Calvary. The Passion Narratives of the Gospels provide the details of our Lord's passion, which are, at least to some extent, corroborated by contemporary Roman historians Tacitus, Seutonius, and Pliny the Younger. Archeological discoveries, combined with modern medical examination, provide an accurate picture of what our Lord endured. In an age in which the "risen" Jesus appears on the cross and *suffering* and *sacrifice* have become unpopular terms, we must not lose sight of the brutal reality of the Passion.

After the Last Supper, Jesus went to the Garden of Gethsemane at the Mount of Olives. Our Lord prayed, "Father, if you are willing, take this cup away from me; still, not my will but yours be done" (Lk 22:42). Jesus knew the sacrifice he faced. He prayed so intensely that "his sweat became like drops of blood falling on the ground" (Lk 22:44). Medical science testifies that people may emit a bloody sweat when in a highly emotional state (a condition called *hematidrosis* or *hemohidrosis*), the result of hemorrhaging into the sweat glands. Little wonder the Father sent an angel to strengthen him (see Lk 22:43). Archbishop Fulton Sheen reflected:

> What was predominant in His mind was not physical pain, but moral evil or sin. . . . In addition to His human intellect, which

had grown by experience, he had the infinite intellect of God which knows all things and sees the past and the future as present. . . . What Our Blessed Lord contemplated in this agony was not just the buffeting of soldiers, and the pinioning of His hands and feet to a bar of contradiction, but rather the awful burden of the world's sin, and the fact that the world was about to spurn His Father by rejecting Him, His Divine Son. (*Life of Christ*, p. 378)

Our Lord was then arrested and tried before the Sanhedrin, presided over by the High Priest Caiaphas. Responding to their questions, he proclaimed, "From now on you will see the 'Son of Man seated at the right hand of the Power' and 'coming on the clouds of heaven'" (Mt 26:64). For this statement, he was condemned to death for blasphemy, and was then spat upon, slapped, and mocked. While the Sanhedrin could condemn our Lord to death, it lacked the authority to execute; only Pontius Pilate, the Roman governor, could order an execution.

The Jewish leaders, therefore, took Jesus to Pilate. Notice how the charge changed: The Jewish leaders told Pilate, "We found this man misleading our people; he opposes the payment of taxes to Caesar and maintains that he is the Messiah, a king" (Lk 23:2). What happened to the charge of blasphemy? Pilate did not care if Jesus wanted to be a messiah, a prophet, or a religious leader; however, if Jesus wanted to be a king, he threatened the authority of Caesar. Any act of rebellion, treason, or subversion had to be punished quickly and severely. So Pilate asked, "Are you the king of the Jews?" (Lk 23:3).

Pilate could not find conclusive evidence to condemn Jesus. Pilate challenged the chief priests, the ruling class, and the people, "I have conducted my investigation in your presence and have not found this man guilty of the charges you have brought against him" (Lk 23:14). When offering to release a prisoner, Pilate asked the crowd about Jesus: "What evil has this man done? I found him guilty of no capital crime" (Lk 23:22). Even Pilate's wife pleaded with him not to interfere in the case of "that righteous man" (Mt 27:19).

Pilate then had Jesus scourged (see Jn 19:1). The Romans used a short whip (*flagrum* or *flagellum*) with several single or braided leather thongs. Iron balls or hooks made of bones or shells were placed at various intervals along the thongs and at their ends. The person was stripped of his clothing and whipped along the back, buttocks, and legs. The scourging ripped the skin and tore into the underlying muscles, leaving the flesh in bloody ribbons. The victim verged on circulatory shock, and the blood loss would help determine how long he would survive on the cross. (Evidence from

the Shroud of Turin indicates that Jesus had 120 wounds from the scourging, resulting from 40 lashes.)

To intensify the suffering, the soldiers added other tortures: crowning him with thorns, dressing him in a purple cloak, placing a reed in his right hand, spitting upon him, and mocking him, "Hail, King of the Jews!" (Mt 27:29). (Pollen evidence from the Shroud of Turin posits that the crown of thorns came from *Gundelia tournefortii*, a thistle-like plant with thorny leaves. This would have been woven into a cap, thereby producing the forty puncture wounds from the mid-forehead to the back of the neck shown on the Shroud of Turin.)

After the scourging, Pilate again presented Christ to the crowd, who chanted, "Crucify him, crucify him!" Fearing a revolt, Pilate capitulated and handed over Jesus to be crucified. The Romans had perfected crucifixion, which probably originated in Persia, to produce a slow death with the maximum amount of pain. Crucifixion was reserved for the worst of criminals. This punishment was so awful that Cicero (d. 43 BC) introduced legislation in the Roman Senate exempting Roman citizens from crucifixion; this is why St. Paul was beheaded rather than crucified for being a Christian.

The victim carried his own cross to further weaken him. Since the entire cross weighed around 300 pounds, he usually carried only the horizontal beam (*patibulum*) (75–125 pounds) to the place of execution where the vertical beams (*stipes*) were already in place. A military guard headed by a centurion led the procession. A soldier carried the *titulus* which displayed the victim's name and his crime, and which was later attached to the cross (see Mt 27:37). For our Lord, the path from the praetorium to Golgotha was about one-third of a mile, and he was so weak that Simon of Cyrene was forced to assist him (see Mt 27:32).

Upon arriving at the place of execution, the law mandated the victim be given a bitter drink of wine mixed with myrrh (gall) as an analgesic (see Mt 27:34). The victim was then stripped of his garments (unless this had already occurred). His hands were stretched over the *patibulum* and either tied, nailed, or both. Archeological evidence reveals the nails were tapered iron spikes approximately seven inches in length with a square shaft about three-eighths of an inch. The nails were driven through the wrist between the radius and the ulna to support the weight of the person. The *patibulum* was affixed to the *stipes*, and the feet were then tied or nailed directly to it or to a small footrest (*suppedaneum*).

As the victim hung on the cross, the crowds commonly tormented him with jeers (cf. Mt 27:39–44). The Romans oftentimes forced the family to watch to add psychological suffering. The soldiers divided the man's garments as part of their reward (see Mt 27:35). The victim would hang on the cross anywhere from three hours to even three days. As he hung in agony, insects would feed on the open wounds or the eyes, ears, and nose, and birds in turn would prey on the victim. With the combined effects caused by the loss of blood, the trauma of scourging, and dehydration, the weight of the body pulled down on the outstretched arms and shoulders, impeding respiration. Most likely, pericardial edema ensued. In all, the person died from a slow asphyxiation. Perhaps this is why Jesus spoke only tersely from the cross. If the person tried to lift himself up on his feet to breathe, incredible pain would be felt in the hands and feet from the nail wounds and in the back from those left by the scourging.

To hasten death, the soldiers would break the legs of the victim, as they did to the two thieves (see Jn 19:32–33). Although Jesus was already dead, the soldiers made sure of the fact by piercing his heart with a lance or sword; when Jesus's heart was pierced, out flowed blood and water (pericardial fluid) (see Jn 19:34).

Upon death, the corpse was sometimes left on the cross until decomposed or eaten by birds or animals as a further sign of what happens to those who rebel against Rome. Most of the time, the corpse was taken down, marked, and placed in a mass grave; after one year, the family could claim the body. However, Roman law allowed the family to take the body for burial with permission of the Roman governor. In our Lord's case, Joseph of Arimathea asked Pilate for Christ's body, and he was then buried (see Jn 19:38).

As we contemplate Holy Week, we must remember what our Lord endured for our salvation. He offered himself as the perfect sacrifice for sin on the altar of the cross and washed away our sins with his blood. We also must recognize our responsibility for sin and the need to repent. The *Catechism* (no. 598), quoting the old *Roman Catechism*, asserts, "Sinners were the authors and the ministers of all the sufferings that the divine Redeemer endured. . . . Since our sins made the Lord Christ suffer the torment of the cross, those who plunge themselves into disorders and crimes crucify the Son of God anew in their hearts (for he is in them) and hold him up to contempt."

Yes, our crucified Lord on the cross is a vivid image of his love for each of us, but one which also reminds us of the horrors of sin. Meditating on his passion will strengthen us against temptation, move us to frequent confession, and keep us on the path of salvation. By embracing our crucified Lord and his cross, we will come to the glory of the resurrection.

A Meditation

For some, the cross marked the end of Jesus. Pilate washed his hands of this political problem between Rome and the Jews, and the possible threat to the authority of Caesar. Although Pilate knew that Jesus was innocent, he did not care. After all, "What is truth?" he asked (Jn 18:38). For him, what was the life of one Jew compared to the preservation of Rome's authority? He thought the crucifixion of our Lord was an end to his problems, at least for a time.

Annas and Caiaphas, and the Jewish elders, also thought this was an end to the would-be Messiah. No longer would he or anyone challenge their authority. He may have driven the money changers and the merchants from the temple, but now, with him hanging on a cross, any threat of him doing the same to them had been removed. Their position was secure. And what if he was innocent? Better for one innocent man to die rather than for the whole nation be destroyed (see Jn 11:50).

Finally, to the crowd, Jesus was just another passing phenomenon. They shouted, "Hosanna in the highest," on Palm Sunday, and then "Crucify him! Crucify him!" on Good Friday.

But we know that the cross was not an end. The cross is a sign of victory. The cross is the means of salvation. The suffering and death on the cross would give way to the resurrection. Through his cross and resurrection, Jesus has set us free: free from sin, suffering, and death. He has established a kingdom of life, truth, and justice to be lived now in freedom and fulfilled in heaven. St. Paul rightly said, "The message of the cross is foolishness to those who are perishing, but to us who are being saved it is the power of God" (1 Cor 1:18).

So when we look at a crucifix, we see victory. First, there is the victory of forgiveness: As Isaiah had prophesied, Jesus was pierced for our offenses, crushed for our sins; upon him was the chastisement that made us whole. Yes, only Jesus, true God who became also true man, could take on the burden of sin for all time and offer the sacrifice that transcends time to forgive sin, including our own.

On this Good Friday, we must not forget that our sins—in that same timeless way—crucify our Lord; he suffers for our sins. For all our sins of pride, he was crowned with thorns; for our sins of gluttony, he thirsted; for our sins of anger, nails were pounded through his hands and feet; for our sins of envy, a mocking title, "King of the Jews," was given; for our sins of greed, he was stripped; for our sins of lust, he was scourged; for our sins of sloth, he carried the cross, falling three times, but each time getting up again. Yes, our sins crucified him.

Yet, as St. Paul said, that cross was a throne of grace and mercy (see Heb 4:16). On that cross, Jesus said, "Father forgive them, for they know not what they are doing." He said to the good thief, "This day you will be with me in paradise." And through the sacrament of Penance, he still says to each of us, "I absolve you from your sins." For all of us members of the struggling Church Militant here on earth, every time we repent, go to confession, and receive absolution, we show the victory of the cross. Likewise, when we forgive, we put a limit on the evil that has hurt us and allow the grace of the Lord to heal the wound in our own soul. Truly it can be said that the forgiveness of the cross conquers all evil.

Second, there is the victory of life. Jesus suffered tremendously and died. He can sympathize with our sufferings. Looking to Jesus, we unite our sufferings to his and offer them for the atonement of our sins, for the souls in purgatory, for the conversion of sinners, or for the sins of this world. Uniting our own suffering to that of our Lord gives it purpose, gives it meaning, so that doing so becomes an act of love that unites us with him.

Moreover, no matter what we suffer, we have the hope of everlasting life with our Lord. I remember an elderly lady I met through my dear friend Bishop Curlin; her name was Dot, for Dorothy. She had suffered cancer of the throat and mouth. She could not talk; she had to use a chalk board. She could not eat and was fed through a feeding tube. Sometimes blood would seep from her mouth. When I last saw her, years ago, Bishop Curlin had Mass for her in her room with her family, who took care of her. She was holding a crucifix. As we offered the Mass, I thought of her being united with Christ, and I thought of the love of her family who suffered with her. When we were leaving, she had written, "I love Jesus." She died soon afterwards. Her noble and beautiful approach to her own suffering and death showed the victory of the cross.

Finally, there is the victory of truth and justice. At times, we face injustice—prejudice or racism, persecution, economic injustice, being passed over or forgotten, having faced some abuse. Life is not fair. We could easily lose hope and despair or become cynical or discouraged if we depended upon truth and justice from political, economic, and social powers. When we look at the cross, however, we see love, the love that Jesus has for each one of us. Jesus says to each one of us, "I love you. And in my kingdom truth and justice will prevail." This, for the Christian, is the victory of the cross.

So, this Good Friday, let us celebrate the victory of God's love for us. But to do so, we must embrace the cross. Jesus said, "Whoever wishes to come after me must deny himself, take up his cross, and follow me" (Mk 8:34). As we venerate the cross during the Liturgy of the Pasion, let us not give the kiss of Judas, but rather the kiss of the disciple who says, "Jesus, I love you. I will follow you. I will bear my cross by repenting of my sin, by uniting my sufferings with yours, and pursuing the course of justice and truth." If we embrace the cross, we will find victory. We will find peace and freedom.

Why the Cross?

In the mid-1930s near Orleans, France, three French boys were fooling around. For some reason, they thought they would play a trick on the parish priest who was hearing confessions. They decided that they would each go to confession and tell the worst possible sins they could think of. For them, the plot was even funnier because one of the boys was a Jew. So they went to the church. The other boys had the little Jewish boy go first. He went to confession, telling the worst possible sins he could think of. The priest, though, knew that something was wrong. So he told the little boy, "For your penance, I want you to go out, stand in front of the big crucifix, look Jesus in the eye, and say five times, 'I don't give a damn that you are hanging on that cross.' Do you promise?" The little boy said, "Yes." Mindful of his promise, the little Jewish boy went out, stood before the life-sized crucifix, fixed his eyes on Jesus, and said, "I don't give a damn that you are hanging on that cross." He said it again, but this time much more timidly. Then he paused. Then his head fell and he looked down. He lifted his head, fixed his eyes on Jesus and said, "I don't. . . ," and his voice cracked. His head fell, he looked down, tears welled up in his eyes. He gulped. He looked up again and said, "Why, why are you hanging on that cross?"

Yes, why? Why, Jesus, are you hanging on the cross? That is the question we ask on Good Friday. Of course, from the earliest catechism class, we learned that Jesus died on the cross to forgive our sins. With a more mature faith, we ponder that sin entered this world. Adam and Eve, our first parents, freely rebelled against God's commandments and will, and sinned. Sin entered this world and sin continued to grow. For the Jewish people, sin was atoned for and forgiven through blood sacrifice. Blood was the life force of the person. The covenant, that bonding of life and love between God and his people, was sealed with the blood of circumcision.

Sin, then, was also in the blood. Through blood sacrifice, sin was forgiven. Through blood sacrifice, the covenant was made and was renewed. With this in mind, St. Paul taught, "Christ ransomed us from the curse of the law by becoming a curse for us, for it is written, 'Cursed be everyone who is hanged on a tree,' that the blessing of Abraham might be extended to the Gentiles through Christ Jesus, so that we might receive the promise of the Spirit through faith" (Gal 3:13–14). Therefore, sin entered the world and entered the "blood" of man when he ate of the forbidden fruit of the Tree of Good and Evil in the Garden of Eden; sin is forgiven through the blood sacrifice of Jesus, the Son of Man, on the cross, the Tree of Life.

Remember the Passover sacrifice: The Jews were slaves in Egypt; God commanded Moses to have the people offer a one-year-old, unblemished male lamb in sacrifice; the Angel of Death passed over the homes marked by the blood but took the lives of those first born males not protected. Because of that blood sacrifice, the Jewish people were freed from slavery, from the sinful land of Egypt, and led to the promised land.

Jesus is the new Passover Lamb. St. John the Baptist proclaimed as he saw Jesus approach, "Behold, the Lamb of God, who takes away the sin of the world" (Jn 1:29). On Good Friday, at the very time the priests in the Temple were slaughtering the lambs for the Passover Supper celebrated that evening, our holy and unblemished Lord was crucified. When he died, none of his bones were broken, unlike that of the two thieves, whose death was hastened by the breaking of their legs (see Jn 19:31ff). Accordingly, St. Peter wrote, "you were ransomed from your futile conduct, handed on by your ancestors, not with perishable things like silver or gold but with the precious blood of Christ as of a spotless unblemished lamb" (1 Pt 1:18–19). Also, in Revelation, St. John has a vision of the heavenly Jerusalem, seeing God, the Father, on the throne, and on the altar, the Lamb (i.e., Jesus) surrounded by the angels and saints, who cried out, "Worthy is the Lamb that was slain to receive power and riches, wisdom and strength, honor and glory and blessing" (Rv 5:12).

Remember also Yom Kippur, the Day of Atonement. On this day, the High Priest would offer the sacrifice to atone for sin: a bull for himself and his family and a goat of all of the people for the whole year. This was the one time of the year that he would enter the Holy of Holies, the inner room of the temple. This room was a perfect cube, thirty feet on each side. There were no windows and a veil, thirty feet by thirty feet, covered the entry way. The Jewish historian Josephus reported that the veil was four inches thick and made of linen and blue, purple, and scarlet yarn with images of cherubim embroidered on it. Inside the Holy of Holies was the Ark of the Covenant, which held the Ten Commandments, the priestly staff of Aaron, and some of the manna from the Exodus journey (see Heb 9:4). On top of the ark was a gold plate: this was the "mercy seat" or "propitiatory" upon which the blood of the Yom Kippur sacrifices would be sprinkled (see Lv 16).

On the Day of Atonement, the High Priest offered the sacrifices. He took the blood of the bull and then of the goat and passed through the veil. He sprinkled the propitiatory with the blood. He pronounced the holy name of God, Yahweh. Through this blood sacrifice, the sins of the Jewish people were washed away. The covenant was renewed. They were made "at one" with God, hence the atonement.

Jesus makes the perfect atonement for our sins. Like the High Priest who entered the Holy of Holies alone, Jesus as the true High Priest offers himself as the sacrifice for sin. He, true God, became also true man. Only he could possibly take the burden of all sin for all time and offer the perfect sacrifice that transcends time. However, since sin entered this world through man, man had to atone for sin. Jesus, true God who became true man, is the High Priest. He is the Lamb of Sacrifice. He is "the living bread come down from heaven." He is the Word of God incarnate, fulfilling all of the commandments and prophecies, and perfectly revealing the truth and love of God. By his blood sacrifice on the altar of the cross, sin was washed away, the new and eternal covenant was made. Keep in mind that unlike the sacrifices of the Old Testament, Christ rose from the dead on Easter morning, conquering sin, suffering, death, and evil. Through his death and resurrection, we have been freed from the slavery of the sin, reconciled to the Father, and given the hope of heaven, the new Promised Land.

For this reason, when our Lord died, the veil was torn in two from top to bottom (see Mt 27:51). This was an action of God. The heavenly Father ripped the veil from top to bottom to proclaim that we no longer had to look to the blood of lambs, goats, and bulls; instead, we only had to look at the cross and see the Savior of the World.

As for the little Jewish boy who asked, "Why are you hanging on that cross?" He was Jean-Marie Lustiger (1926–2007), who was baptized in 1940, became a priest, and eventually was appointed the cardinal archbishop of Paris. He knew the real answer to the question: "God so loved the world that he gave his only Son, so that everyone who believes in him might not perish but might have eternal life" (Jn 3:16).

The Latin Cross and the Eastern Cross

The cross with which most Roman Catholics are familiar is technically termed the "Latin Cross," which has the long vertical beam crossed about two-thirds up by a horizontal beam. This type of cross is believed to be the one upon which the Romans crucified our Lord, nailing his outstretched hands to the ends of the horizontal beam and his feet to the lower portion of the vertical beam.

In the Eastern Rites of our Catholic Church and in the Orthodox Churches, a tradition developed of adding a shorter horizontal beam above the one holding the arms, and at the bottom of the cross, a lower slanted beam. This type of cross is commonly called the "Eastern Cross."

The smaller upper beam represents Pontius Pilate's inscription written in Latin, Greek, and Hebrew: Jesus the Nazorean, the King of the Jews (see Jn 19:19). In Latin, the inscription reads, "*Iesus Nazarenus Rex Iudaeorum,*" which is simply reduced to INRI on most replicas.

The lower beam represents the footrest upon which our Lord's feet were nailed. Several traditions exist which explain the slanting. In the sixth century, the slanted beam symbolized the agony and struggle of our Lord during his suffering on the cross. The Gospel of St. Matthew reads, "Jesus cried out again in a loud voice, and gave up his spirit. And behold, the veil of the sanctuary was torn in two from top to bottom. The earth quaked, rocks were split, tombs were opened" (Mt 27:50–52). At the traumatic climax when he gave up his spirit, the horizontal beam jerked from its horizontal position to the slanting position.

A tradition arising around the eleventh century holds that the slanting beam symbolized the balance between the good thief and the bad thief: the good thief, known as St. Dismas, found salvation at the last moment of his life and would be raised up to heaven, while the bad thief, cursing God in his last breath, would be thrust downward to hell.

In all, whether we reverence the traditional Latin cross or the Eastern cross, we remember the sacrifice our Lord endured for our salvation, and we pray, "We adore you, O Christ, and we praise you, because by your holy cross you have redeemed the world."

Five Uncommon Saints

On Good Friday, the uncommon saints appear in the Passion Narratives and the Stations of the Cross: St. Dismas, St. Longinus, St. Veronica, St. Joseph of Arimathea, and St. Simon of Cyrene. Most of the following relies on tradition rather than the brief mentions the Gospels provide.

ST. DISMAS

The Gospel of St. Luke presents the following account: "One of the criminals hanging reviled Jesus, saying, 'Are you not the Messiah? Save yourself and us.' The other, however, rebuking him, said in reply, 'Have you no fear of God, for you are subject to the same condemnation? And indeed, we have been condemned justly, for the sentence we received corresponds to our crimes, but this man has done nothing criminal.' Then he said, "Jesus, remember me when you come into your kingdom.' He replied to him, 'Amen, I say to you, today you will be with me in Paradise'" (Lk 23:39–43). The Gospel of St. Matthew only states, "The revolutionaries who were crucified with him also kept abusing him in the same way" (27:44).

From these few verses, we know the following: First, others were crucified with our Lord, which would fit the Roman methodology of execution. Second, the "thieves" were more than thieves; they were probably insurgents who were involved in some threat or action against Roman rule since only such a crime would result in crucifixion. Note that for this reason the Jewish leaders changed the charge against our Lord from blasphemy to his claiming to be king of the Jews when he was brought to Pilate; only the latter charge would result in crucifixion. Third, one thief blasphemed our Lord, while the other one made a confession of faith and thereby was welcomed into heaven.

In tradition, the "good thief" has been named St. Dismas, and the "bad thief," Gestas. (Note that Sister Anne Catherine Emmerich, in her visions of the passion, recorded the name of the "bad thief" as "Gestas," which was also used in the movie *The Passion of the Christ*.)

A story that circulated in the early Church relates how the Holy Family encountered these two thieves on their journey to Egypt when fleeing the wrath of King Herod. Moved with compassion, Dismas wanted to leave the Holy Family unharmed, but Gestas wanted to rob and hurt them. So Dismas bribed Gestas with forty drachmas to leave them in peace. The Blessed Mother said to Dismas, "The Lord God shall sustain you with his right hand and give you remission of sins." Thereupon, the Infant Jesus added, "After thirty years, mother, the Jews will crucify me in Jerusalem, and these two robbers will be lifted on the cross with me, Dismas on my right hand, Gestas on my left, and after that day, Dismas shall go before me into Paradise." This pious story is found in the apocryphal "Gospel of the Infancy," which lacks apostolic foundation. Variations of the story also use different names for the thieves, but "Dismas" and "Gestas" were predominantly used in the West.

Nevertheless, St. Dismas's feast day is March 25, and the Roman Martyrology announces the feast day with this proclamation: "At Jerusalem the commemoration of the holy thief who confessed Christ upon the cross and deserved to hear from Him the words: 'This day shalt thou be with me in paradise.'"

ST. LONGINUS

St. Longinus, a Roman centurion, was charged with the crucifixion of our Lord. To make sure Jesus was dead, he pierced his side: "One soldier thrust his lance into his side, and immediately blood and water flowed out" (Jn 19:34). He proclaimed, "Truly this man was the Son of God!" (Mk 15:39).

In her visions, Sister Anne Catherine Emmerich recorded this event, adding that when St. Longinus pierced the heart of our Lord, blood and water covered his face and body. She wrote, "Grace and salvation at once entered his soul. He leaped from his horse, threw himself upon his knees, struck his breast, and confessed loudly before all his firm belief in the divinity of Jesus." Moreover, he was miraculously cured of failing eyesight. According to the visions, Mary, St. John, the holy women, and the soldier gathered up the blood and water in flasks, and soaked up the remainder with linen cloths.

Sister Anne Catherine identified the Roman soldier as "Cassius" (also used in the movie *The Passion of the Christ*). She noted, "Cassius was baptized by the name Longinus; and was ordained deacon, and preached the faith. He always kept some of the blood of Christ—it dried up, but was found in his coffin in Italy. He was buried in a town at no great distance from the locality where St. Clare passed her life. There is a lake with an island upon it near this town, and the body of Longinus must have been taken there" (*The Dolorous Passion of Our Lord Jesus Christ*, ch. 48). The

locality mentioned is Mantua, and tradition holds that St. Longinus suffered martyrdom there.

Blessed James of Voragine (d. 1298) in his *Golden Legend,* which contains a collection of stories about the saints, although some more of popular piety than historical fact, tells another version of St. Longinus's martyrdom. In Caesarea of Cappadocia (modern day Turkey), he was arrested for being a Christian. He was famous for his preaching and converting many to Christianity. When he refused to offer sacrifice to the pagan gods, the Roman governor ordered Longinus's teeth knocked-out and his tongue cut off, but miraculously he could still speak in defense of the faith. He even smashed the statues of the pagan idols. The governor then ordered the beheading of Longinus. Seeing his courage and goodness, the governor repented.

St. Longinus's feast day is October 16. Interestingly, the relic of St. Longinus's lance is preserved at St. Peter's in Rome, having been presented to Pope Innocent VIII in 1492 by the Turkish Sultan Bajazet; some of the sacred relics had fallen into the hands of the Muslims when they conquered Jerusalem and Constantinople.

ST. VERONICA

The Sixth Station of the Way of the Cross is "Veronica wipes the face of Jesus." Who is this Veronica? She is not mentioned in the Gospels. Tradition holds that she was a pious and wealthy matron in Jerusalem. Some traditions, albeit spurious, identity her as the woman who had suffered the hemorrhages and was cured by Jesus (Mk 5:25–34).

Nevertheless, she took pity on our Lord as he carried his cross to Calvary. She fulfilled the Lord's own teaching, "Whatever you did for one of these least brothers of mine, you did for me" (Mt 25:40). She had the courage to step out of the crowd and perform

a simple task, but a task of great compassion: she wiped the sweat and blood from our Lord's face. As Pope Benedict wrote in his Stations of the Cross, "She did not let herself be deterred by the brutality of the soldiers or the fear which gripped the disciples. She is the image of that good woman, who, amid turmoil and dismay, shows the courage born of goodness and does not allow her heart to be bewildered."

Jesus left the image of his holy face on the veil. St. Veronica kept the veil, which soon became known for its miraculous powers. Shortly thereafter, Emperor Tiberius (who ruled AD 14–37) summoned Veronica to Rome. Tiberius was suffering from a serious malady and remembered hearing of the veil's powers during a previous visit to Jerusalem. After her arrival, he was cured by touching the sacred image.

Veronica stayed in Rome and was acquainted with St. Peter and St. Paul. Upon her death, she bequeathed the veil to Pope St. Clement (who reigned AD 88–99).

The veil has been kept at St. Peter's Basilica in Rome. Since the early 1620s, the veil has been displayed only once a year, on the Fifth Sunday of Lent during Solemn Vespers from the balcony atop St. Veronica's column in St. Peter's.

Pope Benedict said, "Yet her act of love impressed the true image of Jesus on her heart: on His human face, bloodied and bruised, she saw the face of God and His goodness, which accompanies us even in our deepest sorrows. Only with the heart can we see Jesus. Only love purifies us and gives us the ability to see. Only love enables us to recognize the God who is love itself." The name *Veronica* means "true icon." Like Veronica, may we see Jesus and recognize his presence in others. In turn, may we be true icons of Jesus so that others may recognize Jesus through us. St. Veronica's feast day is July 12.

ST. JOSEPH OF ARIMATHEA

Joseph, a wealthy Jew from the town of Arimathea, was "a virtuous and righteous man" (Lk 23:50). He was not part of the plot to kill Jesus. Rather, he was a disciple (see Mt 28:57) who looked forward to the reign of God (see Mk 15:43; Lk 23:51). However, Joseph was "secretly a disciple of Jesus for fear of the Jews" (Jn 19:38).

After our Lord was crucified, he was bold enough to ask Pilate for the body of Jesus (see Mk 15:43), and Pilate granted the request. The body of Jesus was taken down from the cross, wrapped in fine linen, and placed in Joseph's new, never used tomb, hewn out of rock (see Lk 23:52).

Stories circulating in the Middle Ages relate that St. Joseph accompanied St. Philip to Gaul to preach the Gospel. He then headed a mission to England. There he established a chapel in honor of our Blessed Mother, which eventually became Glastonbury Abbey. A final story is that St. Joseph was given custody of the Lord's chalice used at the Last Supper, "the Holy Grail." Again we can turn to Pope Benedict XVI who, in his meditation on the Thirteenth Station, said Joseph was "a rich man who is able to pass

through the eye of a needle, for God had given him the grace," a reference to our Lord's famous teaching about the danger of riches: "It is easier for a camel to pass through the eye of a needle than for one who is rich to enter the kingdom of God" (Mt 19:24).

ST. SIMON OF CYRENE

In addressing St. Simon of Cyrene, we must realize that we face a puzzling character. He is not listed on the calendar of saints in either the Catholic Church or the Orthodox Churches, nor is he mentioned as a saint in books like *Butler's Lives of the Saints* or both the new and old editions of *The Catholic Encyclopedia*. However, parishes have been named after him; for example, St. Simon of Cyrene Church in St. Louis, Missouri. Since there was no universal canonization process in the early Church, public acclamation sufficed. Also, anyone who is in heaven is recognized as a saint, even if not officially canonized. Whatever the case, the figure of Simon of Cyrene, remembered in the Fifth Station of the Cross, provides a good meditation for all of us.

As Jesus carried the cross, the Romans pressed into service Simon, a Cyrenian who was coming in from the fields (see Mt 27:32; Lk 23:26.) They probably feared that our Lord, beaten and scourged, would die before arriving at Calvary. Cyrene is located in present day Libya, and in ancient times had a large Jewish community. These Jews also established their own synagogue in Jerusalem, where they went during the special feasts, like Passover.

St. Mark added that Simon was the father of Alexander and Rufus (Mk 15:21). Their mention in the Gospel suggests that they were members of the early Christian community. Some speculated that Rufus is the person of the same name mentioned by St. Paul in his Letter to the Romans (16:13).

Lastly, another speculation is that Simon and his sons were among "the men of Cyrene" who preached the Gospel to the Greeks in Antioch (see Acts 11:19ff).

Pope Benedict, in his meditation on the Fifth Station, wrote,

> From this chance encounter, faith was born. The Cyrenian, walking beside Jesus and sharing the burden of the Cross, came to see that it was a grace to be able to accompany him to his crucifixion and to help him. The mystery of Jesus, silent and suffering, touched Simon's heart. Jesus, whose divine love alone can redeem all his humanity, wants us to share his Cross so that we can complete what is still lacking in his suffering. Whenever we show kindness to the suffering, the persecuted and defenseless, and share in their sufferings, we help carry that same Cross of Jesus. In this way, we hope to obtain salvation, and help contribute to the salvation of the world.

Like Simon, we may never be canonized—that is, formally declared a saint—but we must strive for holiness and hope to be welcomed into the communion of saints in heaven.

Although some mystery surrounds these saints, their importance is found in the role they played in the passion of our Lord. All of them inspire us by their example and give us the hope of salvation.

Hot Cross Buns

A monk at St. Alban's Abbey in England is credited with introducing the hot cross bun for Good Friday in the 1300s. These buns were made from the same dough as altar bread and marked with a cross on top. They were then given to the poor to provide some sustenance on a day of fasting.

When the fasting laws were relaxed, hot cross buns were made of a sweet and spiced dough (to symbolize the herbs and spices used in our Lord's burial) and topped with a cross of white icing. Some versions also add raisins soaked in brandy to the dough to symbolize the bread and wine offered at the Last Supper.

Although Friday is a day of fast and abstinence from meat, whereby a person is allowed only one full meal during the day and a snack or two to keep strength, a hot cross bun may be a good source for a snack. Also, these buns were traditionally not only enjoyed by the family but also distributed to the poor.

Holy Saturday Morning and the Blessing of Food

On Holy Saturday, we wait in expectation. An ancient homily for Holy Saturday reads, "Something strange is happening—there is a great silence on earth today, a great silence and stillness. The whole earth keeps silence because the King is asleep. The earth trembles and is still because God has fallen asleep in the flesh and he has raised up all who have slept ever since the world began. God has died in the flesh and hell trembles with fear." We believe that our Lord descended to the Land of the Dead, Sheol, to reveal himself to the faithful who had been awaiting a Messiah and Redeemer and then took them into heaven.

On Holy Saturday morning, particularly in Eastern European countries, the faithful bring their baskets of food—decorated eggs, breads, meats, wine, etc.—that will be enjoyed on Easter to be blessed by the priest.

Descended into Hell?

This phrase of the Creed—Jesus "descended into hell"—causes confusion. When we hear the word *hell*, we immediately think of the place of eternal damnation for those who have rejected God in this life and have committed mortal sins without repentance.

The problem is one of translation: Our English word *hell* is used to translate the Hebrew *sheol*, which denoted "the place of the dead." (Interestingly, the English word *hell* is derived from a Germanic name for the place of the dead in Teutonic mythology.) *Sheol* was the netherworld, for both the good and the bad, the just and the unjust. In the later writings of the Old Testament, a clear distinction is made between where the good resided as opposed to where the bad did, with the two separated by an impassable abyss. The section for the unjust was later named *Gehenna*, where the souls would suffer eternal torment by fire.

Our Lord attested to this "land of the dead" understanding of hell. Recall the parable of Lazarus, the poor beggar, who sat at the gate of the rich man, traditionally called Dives (see Lk 16:19ff). Lazarus dies and is taken to the "land of the dead" (the original Greek text uses the word *hades*, which was used to translate *sheol*) and is comforted at the bosom of Abraham. Dives also dies and goes to the "land of the dead"; however, he finds eternal torment, being tortured in flames. Moreover, a great abyss separates the two sides of *sheol*.

Given this understanding, we believe that the sin of Adam and Eve had closed the gates of heaven. The holy souls awaited the Redeemer in the land of the dead; that is, *sheol*. Our Lord offered the perfect sacrifice for all sin by dying on the cross, the redemptive act that touches all people of every time—past, present and future. His sacrifice is the perfect act of love. He was then buried. During that time, he descended among the dead. His soul, separated from his body, joined the holy souls awaiting the Savior in that Land of the Dead. His descent among them brought to completion the proclamation of the Gospel and liberated those holy souls—like Adam and Eve, Abraham, Moses, and the prophets—who had long awaited their Redeemer. The gates of heaven were now open, and these holy souls entered everlasting happiness, enjoying the beatific vision.

Pope Benedict XVI, in his 2007 Easter Vigil homily, preached:

The liturgy applies to Jesus' descent into the night of death the words of Psalm 24: "Lift up your heads, O gates; be lifted up, O ancient doors!" The gates of death are closed, no one can return from there. There is no key for those iron doors. But Christ has the key. His Cross opens wide the gates of death, the stern doors. They are barred no longer. His Cross, His radical love, is the key that opens them. The love of the One who, though God, became man in order to die—this love has the power to open those doors. This love is stronger than death. . . . Entering the world of the dead, Jesus bears the stigmata, the signs of His passion: His wounds, His suffering, have become power: they are love that conquers death. He meets Adam and all the men and women waiting in the night of death. . . . In the incarnation, the Son of God became one with human beings—with Adam. But only at this moment, when he accomplishes the supreme act of love by descending into the night of death, does he bring the journey of the incarnation to its completion. By his death he now clasps the hand of Adam, of every man and woman who awaits Him, and brings them to the light.

(Please note Jesus did not deliver those souls damned to eternal punishment in hell nor did he destroy hell as such; unjust souls remained in that state and place of damnation begun at the time of their particular judgment.)

The *Catechism* highlights the importance of this event: "This is the last phase of Jesus' messianic mission, a phase which is condensed in time but vast in its real significance: the spread of Christ's redemptive work to all men of all times and all places, for all who are saved have been made sharers in the redemption" (no. 634).

Blessing of Foods at Easter

A beautiful family tradition among Central and Eastern Europeans is to bring the food prepared for the Easter celebration to church on Saturday morning for a special blessing from the priest. The following is a blessing used at Our Lady of Hope Church, where I am pastor, which was handed onto me from a senior priest friend. (Unfortunately, I do not know the origins of the prayers or the identity of the one who composed them.) If your parish does not offer such a service, the family could conduct their own service of blessing, just as they would before meals.

BLESSING OF MEATS

Father, giver of all good things, You commanded our ancestors in faith to partake of lamb on Passover night. Through Moses You commanded Your people in their deliverance from Egypt to kill a lamb and mark their doorposts with its blood. We understand this to prefigure our deliverance by Jesus' shedding of His blood. +[1] Bless this lamb and other meat prepared for our celebration in

---

1   Indicates the sign of the cross is to be made here.

honor of Your Son's Passover from death to life, for He is truly the Paschal Lamb by Whose blood we are saved, Who lives and reigns for ever and ever. Amen.

BLESSING OF BREAD

Almighty, everlasting God, be pleased to + bless this bread. May it be a healthful food for body and soul, a safeguard against every disease, and a defense against all harm. We ask this through our Lord Jesus Christ, the bread of life, Who came down from heaven and gives life and salvation to all the world, Who lives and reigns for ever and ever. Amen.

BLESSING OF DAIRY FOODS

O God, Creator and Author of all being, **+** bless these cheeses and butter and other dairy foods. Keep us in Your love, so that as we partake of them, we may be filled with your bountiful gifts on account of our Lord's glorious resurrection from the dead. We give glory to You, our Father without beginning, to Your Son, Who is our true Food, and to Your good and life-giving Spirit, now and forever. Amen

BLESSING OF EGGS

Father in heaven, let Your **+** blessing come upon these eggs. When we break them, we see a sign of Your Son rising to new life from the tomb. May we eat them in joyful celebration of His resurrection, for He lives and reigns with You for ever and ever. Amen.

BLESSING OF CAKES AND PASTRIES

Lord Jesus Christ, living bread of everlasting life, **+** bless these cakes and pastries as You once blessed the five loaves in the wilderness. As we eat them, may we receive the health we desire for body and soul. We ask this of You, our risen Lord, Who lives and reigns for ever and ever. Amen.

BLESSING OF WINE

Lord Jesus Christ, Son of the living God, in Cana of Galilee You changed water into wine. Be pleased to **+** bless this wine which You have given us as refreshment. Grant that whenever it is taken as drink, it may be accompanied by an outpouring of Your life-giving grace, for ever and ever. Amen.

BLESSING OF CHILDREN AND THEIR EASTER BASKETS

Loving Father, long ago You told Your people to bring the good things for eating and celebrating to Your altar in thanksgiving. They obeyed and brought You their baskets of food and grain before they ate and celebrated. Today these boys and girls do the same as they come here with their Easter baskets. We ask you to + bless them and their parents and friends. Grant that they and their families may appreciate all that You give them. + Bless their Easter eggs and candy and all that the baskets contain, with which they will celebrate the resurrection of Jesus, Your Son and our brother. As they eat these foods and candies may their Easter joy increase. We ask this through Christ our risen Lord. Amen.

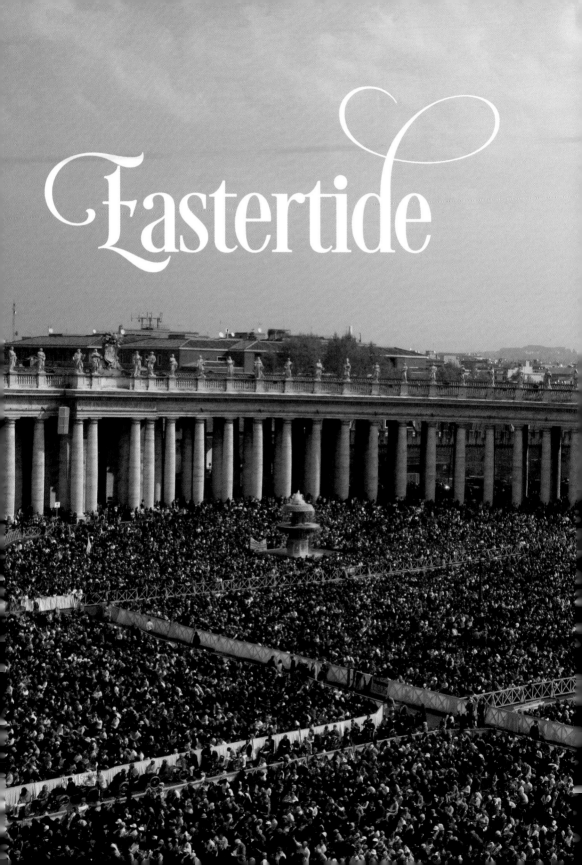

Eastertide

The Easter Vigil

On Holy Saturday evening, the first Mass of Easter, the great Easter Vigil, is celebrated. The Roman Missal describes this as "the greatest and most noble of all solemnities." The faithful gather in darkness. The priest blesses the new fire and the paschal candle, which is then lit and from which the faithful light their candles. The deacon proclaims, "Christ our light," and then sings the beautiful Exsultet. The opening verses set the theme for the Easter celebration: "Exult, let them exult, the hosts of heaven, exult, let Angel ministers of God exult, let the trumpet of salvation sound aloud our mighty King's triumph! Be glad, let earth be glad, as glory floods her, ablaze with light from her eternal King, let all corners of the earth be glad, knowing an end of gloom and darkness. Rejoice, let Mother Church also rejoice, arrayed with the lighting of his glory, let this holy building shake with joy, filled with the mighty voices of the peoples."

During the Liturgy of the Word, a glimpse of salvation history is recounted: five passages and psalms from the Old Testament are read, followed by the Gloria, then the Epistle, the Great Alleluia, and the Gospel. After the homily, the sacraments of Baptism and Confirmation are celebrated, and then the Mass continues with the Liturgy of the Eucharist, with the new members of the Church receiving the Holy Eucharist for the first time. The final blessing of the Easter Vigil concludes the Sacred Triduum. The joyful celebration of Easter has begun!

Easter

Alleluia!

Alleluia or *Halleluiah* is a Hebrew word meaning, "Praise Yahweh." The expression appears throughout the psalms. During the Easter Vigil Mass, after the reading of the Epistle, the priest (or cantor) solemnly intones the Alleluia three times, with each intonation raised a step, with the congregation repeating it. At the end of Mass, the Alleluia is also added: The priest (or deacon) dismisses the people, "Go forth, the Mass is ended, alleluia, alleluia." To which the congregation responds, "Thanks be to God, alleluia, alleluia."

In his book *Dogma and Preaching* (p. 47–48), Pope Benedict reflected:

> Singing indicates that the person is passing beyond the boundaries of the merely rational and falling into a kind of ecstasy; the merely rational he can express in ordinary language (that is why overly rational people are seldom tempted to sing). Now singing

finds its climactic form in the Alleluia, the song in which the very essence of all song achieves its purest embodiment. . . . In fact, we are dealing here with something that cannot be translated. The Alleluia is simply the nonverbal expression in song of a joy that requires no words because it transcends all words.

Therefore, what better word of praise than *Alleluia* can express the joy that the love of God shown through Jesus Christ has conquered falsehood and sin, suffering and death, and evil itself? And so, the Alleluia expresses a joy and praise to God where all other words fail.

One of the most beautiful pieces of music composed and performed during Easter is the "Halleluiah Chorus" of Handel's Messiah. In August 1741, George Frideric Handel (1685–1759) was in the depths of despair. His patroness, Queen Caroline of England, had died and therefore his primary source of income ceased. Wars abroad had forced many of the theaters in London to close, thereby eliminating another source of revenue. With his savings depleted, his creditors pressured him. On some days, he went without enjoying a meal. Even worse, the public had seemed to have forgotten the great musician; people passed him on the streets without even taking notice. Worst of all these miseries, Handel felt that he had lost his creative genius.

One day, walking the streets of London, he felt very much alone and forgotten. He entered his house and lay down, hoping to never wake-up. Just then, he noticed a thick envelope on his desk containing a new libretto from his collaborator Charles Jennings. Handel thought, "What can I do, a forgotten musician?" Nevertheless, he rose from his bed, and he opened the libretto.

He read the opening words, taken from the Prophet Isaiah: "Comfort ye, comfort ye my people, saith your God." An angelic

summons filled his ears. He continued on: "The people that walked in darkness has seen a great light." The dawn of a new day began to dispel the darkness that overwhelmed him. He read on, "For unto us a child is born, a son is given." Reading through the libretto, Handel journeyed through the prophecies of the Old Testament, the birth of the Lord, and then finally his passion, death, and resurrection. The final words were "Hallelujah!" A creative fire was ignited again in his heart.

For three weeks, Handel worked non-stop putting the words to music and produced the magnificent *Messiah*. When he had finished, he said, "I do believe I have seen all of Heaven before me, and the great God Himself." The *Messiah* was ready for its premier performance on Easter 1742. As Handel heard the Halleluiah chorus, tears of joy ran down his cheeks.

After the performance, he was asked, "What do you think?" He said, "I know that my Redeemer lives. I was sick, and now I am cured. I was in prison, and now I am free. I was in darkness, and now I am in light." Truly, Handel could say, "Halleluiah! Christ is risen! And I have risen to new life with him!"

The Date for Easter

In the Western tradition of the Church, Easter has been celebrated on the first Sunday following the new full moon which occurs on or immediately after the vernal, or spring, equinox. This dating was established by the Council of Nicea in AD 325. As such, the dates for Easter may range from March 22 to April 25. (The Orthodox Churches follow a different dating system and will thereby celebrate Easter one, four, or five weeks later.)

The Word *Easter* – Different Languages, Different Words

In the original language of the Gospels, the Greek word *pascha* is used for the Aramaic form of the Hebrew word *pesach*, which means Passover. During the first three centuries of the Church, *Pasch* referred specifically to the celebration of Christ's passion and death; by the end of the fourth century, it also included the Easter Vigil; and by the end of the fifth century, it referred to Easter itself. In all, the term signified Christ as the new Passover Lamb. Together, the mystery of the Last Supper, the sacrifice of Good Friday, and the resurrection of Easter form the new Passover—the new Pasch.

Latin used the Greek-Hebrew root for its word *Pascha* and other derivatives to signify Easter or the Easter mysteries. For instance, the Easter Vigil in Latin is *Sabbato Sancto de Vigilia Paschali* and in the First Preface of Easter, the priest prays, "*Cum Pascha nostrum immolatus est Christus*" ("When Christ our Pasch was sacrificed"). The Romance languages later used the Hebrew-Greek-Latin root for their words denoting Easter: Italian, *Pasqua*; Spanish, *Pascua*; and French, *Paques*. Even some non-Romance languages employ the Hebrew-Greek-Latin root: Scotch, *Pask*; Dutch, *Paschen*; Swedish, *Pask*; and the German dialect along the lower Rhine, *Paisken*.

However, according to St. Bede (d. 735), the great Church historian of England, the title *Easter* seems to have originated in English around the eighth century. The word *Easter* is derived from the word *Eoster*, the name of the Teutonic goddess of the rising light of day and spring, and the annual sacrifices associated with her. If this is the origin of our word *Easter*, then the Church "baptized" the name, using it to denote that first Easter Sunday morning when Christ, our Light, rose from the grave and when the women found the tomb empty just as dawn was breaking.

Another possibility which arises from more recent research suggests the early Church referred to Easter week as *hebdomada alba* ("white week"), from the white garments worn by the newly baptized. Some mistranslated the word to mean "the shining light of day" or "the shining dawn," and therefore used the Teutonic root *eostarun*, the Old German plural for *dawn*, as the basis for the German *Ostern* and for the English equivalent *Easter*. In early English translations of the Bible made by Tyndale and Coverdale, the word *Easter* was substituted for the word *Passover* in some verses.

The Resurrection of the Body

In the Gospels, Jesus had predicted three times that he would be arrested by the chief priests and scribes, suffer, be condemned to death, and be crucified; however, he also predicted that he would be raised up on the third day (cf. Mt 16:21; 17:22–23; 20:17–19). The predictions came true. On Easter Sunday morning, when Mary Magdalene, the other women, St. Peter, and St. John went to the tomb, they found it empty. The angel proclaimed, "You seek Jesus of Nazareth, the crucified. He has been raised; he is not here" (Mk 16:6). Jesus had risen body and soul from the dead.

Later, Jesus appeared to the apostles and others. He would appear and disappear suddenly. He could be embraced (see Mt 28:9). He shows the wound marks of his hands and side to the apostles, and invited St. Thomas to examine them with his fingers (see Jn 20:19ff). He was not always easily recognizable, as in the appearance to Mary Magdalene (see Jn 20:11ff) or to the apostles by the Sea of Galilee (see Jn 21:1ff). Jesus also shared meals with his apostles (see Jn 21:9ff; Lk 24:36ff) and other disciples (see Lk 23:13). However, Jesus affirmed he was not some ghost or some

resuscitated corpse. Jesus said, "Look at my hands and my feet, that it is I myself. Touch me and see, because a ghost does not have flesh and bones as as you can see I have" (Lk 24:39).

Clearly, our Lord appeared bodily, but he was no longer bound to the laws of our time and space. Therefore, through the resurrection, our Lord had a radically transformed or glorified existence. Simply, "glorification" means that Jesus was fully and perfectly spiritualized and divinized without loss of his humanity.

We believe that we too will share this glorification. When we die, our soul stands before God in the particular judgment, and we have to account for our lives—the good and the bad, the omissions and the commissions. God will then judge the soul worthy of heaven, hell, or purgatory.

At the end of time—the time of our Lord's second coming and the general judgment—we too will share in the resurrection of the dead and be reunited with our body. At that time, Christ will transform the body of the righteous and make it like his own glorified body. St. Paul addressed this issue: "Someone may say, 'How are the dead raised? With what kind of body will they come back?' You fool! What you sow is not brought to life unless it dies. . . . So also is the resurrection of the dead. It is sown corruptible; it is raised incorruptible. It is sown dishonorable; it is raised glorious. It is sown weak; it is raised powerful. If there is a natural body, there is also a spiritual one" (1 Cor 15:35–36, 42–44).

The bodies of the faithful will be transfigured to the pattern of the risen Christ. Traditionally, theology has described these resurrected and glorified bodies as having the characteristics of identity, entirety, and immortality. Moreover, they will also have four transcendent qualities: *impassibility*, or freedom from physical evil, death, sickness, and pain; *clarity*, or freedom from defects and an endowment with beauty and radiance; *agility*, whereby the soul moves the body and there is freedom of motion; and *subtility*, whereby the body is completely spiritualized under the dominion of the soul. The *Catechism* teaches, "After the universal judgment, the righteous will reign for ever with Christ, glorified in body and soul" (no. 1042).

What about the resurrected bodies of the souls of the damned in hell? These bodies will have identity, entirety, and immortality, but not the four transcendent qualities. They will have the condition necessary for suffering the eternal punishment of hell, but not the glorification of the Lord shared by those in heaven.

We must admit that this "glorification" exceeds our understanding and even our imagination. Keep in mind that each of us is a person, a union of body and soul, and Christ came to redeem each of us as a whole person. The late great theologian Hans Urs von Balthasar posited, "A bodiless soul is not a human being, and reincarnation would never be able to redeem us from entrapment in death. But this hope, insane in view of decay and the grave, and also contradictory to all experience, hangs on one fact: Christ's Resurrection, apart from which all Christian belief is 'in vain' (1 Cor 15:14)" (*Credo*, 95). Therefore, we believe in this because Christ, who rose body and soul from the dead, promised us a like resurrection of the body: "The hour is coming in which all who are in the tombs will hear his voice and will come out, those who have done good deeds to the resurrection of life; but those who have done wicked deeds to the resurrection of condemnation" (Jn 5:28–29).

Easter Foods, Flowers, and Other Festive Items

Many of the special Easter foods are due to the very strict Lenten fast during which time the faithful abstained from these foods or ingredients. Remember, during Lent, the faithful abstained from all forms of meat (except fish in some areas of the Church) and animal products, including eggs, milk, butter, and fat. For example, Pope St. Gregory (d. 604), writing to St. Augustine of Canterbury, issued the following rule: "We abstain from flesh, meat, and from all things that come from flesh, as milk, cheese, and eggs." Also, churches were not decorated with flowers to remind us of the "desert experience" of forty days.

Decorated eggs dyed in bright colors are a sign of rejoicing. The Eastern European peoples even decorate the eggs with very intricate designs and religious artwork. The Easter egg symbolizes the Resurrection: just as a little chick pecks its way out from the egg shell to emerge to new life, so Christ emerged from the tomb to new and everlasting life. The unbroken egg symbolizes the rock tomb of our Lord; and when broken, symbolizes that he has risen

from the dead. The ancient Romans had a saying, "*Omne vivum ex ovo*" ("All life comes from an egg"); easily, one can see how such a saying would inspire the early Christians to use the egg as an appropriate symbol for the new and everlasting life won for us through our Lord's passion, death, and resurrection.

According to a Ukrainian folktale, on Good Friday when our Lord was crucified, a poor peddler went to the market in Jerusalem to sell his basket of eggs. He witnessed Jesus carrying his heavy cross through the streets, being taunted by the Romans and mocked by the crowd. The Romans pressed the peddler into service—Simon of Cyrene—and he left his basket by the roadside to help Jesus carry the cross. When he returned to retrieve his eggs, he noticed they were transformed, painted with bright colors and beautiful designs. Only after Easter and the resurrection of the Lord did he realize that these eggs were a sign of rebirth for all of mankind. To this day, the Ukrainian people decorate *pysanky* as part of their Easter celebration.

Another story involves St. Mary Magdalene, who stood at the cross with our Blessed Mother and St. John the Apostle on Good Friday, and who saw the Risen Lord on Easter Sunday morning. Shortly after Easter, Tiberius Caesar visited Jerusalem. Many brought the emperor valuable gifts. Mary Magdalene presented an egg, and said, "Christ is risen!" Tiberius said, "It is easier for an egg to turn red than for a man to rise from the dead." With that, the egg turned bright red. Mary proclaimed, "See! Christ shed his blood to forgive our sins and has risen from the dead to give us new life. The tomb is empty."

Lamb also has significance in the Easter celebration, since Jesus is the Lamb of God, the new Passover Lamb, who offered himself as our sacrifice and freed us from the slavery of sin. A special Easter pastry is a cake shaped like a lamb. Butter shaped in the form of a lamb is also a popular tradition. In the Middle Ages, lamb was the customary meat eaten on Easter and was the main meat for the Holy Father's Easter dinner.

New clothing also has special meaning. In the early Church, during the Easter Vigil, those who were baptized wore a white garment, which was worn throughout the entire week of Easter. As our present ritual indicates, this white garment is a sign that the person has been reborn in baptism, freed from sin, filled with grace, and given a new Christian dignity and identity. Although the other faithful, who had already been baptized, did not wear white garments, they customarily wore new clothes to show that they had risen to a new life through the prayer, fasting, and penances of Lent. The white garments and the new clothes were an outward sign of renewal of faith in the Lord.

In Christian iconography, white lilies have always been the symbol of beauty, purity, and holiness. Even in the Gospel of Luke, our Lord referred to the lilies: "Notice how the flowers grow. They do

not toil or spin. But I tell you, not even Solomon in all his splendor was dressed like one of them" (12:27). Quite appropriately, these beautiful, large, white lilies became very popular in the Easter decorations of churches, symbolizing the new life of our Risen Lord and the new life of grace he offers to us.

As an aside, a religious legend did arise concerning the lily: On Holy Thursday evening, when our Lord was in the Garden of Gethsemane, all of the flowers—except the proud, stately, most beautiful lily—bowed their heads in sorrow because of the ordeal our Lord was suffering. In the end, having witnessed our Lord's humility and sacrifice, the lily hung its head in shame, and has humbly done so to this day.

Another legend surrounds the dogwood tree. At the time of Jesus, the dogwood was a large, tall tree, like an oak in size and strength. Because of these qualities, it was chosen for the wood of the cross. The noble dogwood was distressed to have been chosen to participate in such cruelty and injustice. As our Lord hung upon the cross, sensing the sorrow of the dogwood, he said, "Because of your regret and pity for my suffering, never again shall you, oh noble dogwood, grow large enough to be used as a cross. You shall be slender, bent, and twisted. Your blossoms shall be in the form of a cross. In the center and outer edge of each petal, there will be nail prints, brown with rust and stained with red. A crown of thorns will be in the center of the flower. Now all who see it will remember my sacrifice."

What about the Easter bunny? As mentioned previously, the word *Easter* is derived from both the word *Eoster* (also spelled *Eastre*), the name of the Teutonic goddess of the rising light of day and spring, and the annual sacrifices associated with her, and the Teutonic root *eostarun*, the Old German plural for *dawn*. Spring is a season of fertility, life, and abundance. In Teutonic mythology, Eoster's pet bird laid eggs in baskets and hid them. On a whim, Eoster transformed her pet bird into a rabbit, who continued to lay eggs. Rabbits themselves were a pagan symbol of fertility— hence the phrase, "Multiply like rabbits"—and were often kept in homes as pets. From this pagan custom, the folktale of "the Easter bunny" arose in Germany in the Middle Ages.

Finally, how about pineapple upside down cake? Here is an official Saunders family tradition for Easter Sunday dinner: Each Easter, my mother baked a pineapple upside down cake. It is an interesting cake because it is baked in an iron skillet upside down. When finished and cooled, the skillet is inverted and, *voila*, a wonderful cake, with a brown sugar glaze and topped with pineapple rings each dotted in the center with a red maraschino cherry.

My culinary theology suggests that Christ came into a world turned upside down by sin; by his cross and resurrection, he has turned the world right side up and established a kingdom of Grace. The pineapple rings remind us of the dawning of a new day and the rising of the sun on that Easter Sunday morning when Jesus rose from the dead. The red cherry reminds us of the Sacred Heart of our Lord, who shed his blood to forgive our sins and reconcile us with the heavenly Father.

The Easter Duty

The Fourth Lateran Council (1215) had mandated, "Every faithful of either sex who has reached the age of discretion should at least once a year faithfully confess all his sins in secret to his own priest. He should strive as far as possible to fulfill the penance imposed on him, and with reverence receive at least during Easter time the sacrament of the Eucharist." For good reason, this mandate became simply known as "the Easter duty."

In 1983, the *Code of Canon Law* slightly adjusted the stipulations: "After having attained the age of discretion, each of the faithful is bound by an obligation faithfully to confess serious sins at least once a year" (no. 989). Moreover, the *Code* also asserted, "It is to be recommended to the Christian faithful that venial sins also be confessed" (no. 988.2).

For this reason, The *Catechism of the Catholic Church* lists five precepts that are obligatory for the faithful, including, "The second precept ('You shall confess your sins at least once a year.') ensures preparation for the Eucharist by the reception of the sacrament of reconciliation, which continues Baptism's work of conversion and forgiveness" (no. 2042).

Therefore, one could say, "Yes, there is still the Easter duty," while recognizing that one's confession and reception of sacramental absolution for serious sins (i.e., mortal sins) and reception of Holy Communion may occur any time during the year.

What is most important for all of us is to appreciate the spiritual intent behind the Easter duty. First, the precepts of the Church are the minimum standards for a good spiritual life. They seek to integrate the sacramental and moral teachings and provide a basic paradigm to help a person grow in love of God and neighbor.

Second, the Easter duty seeks to prevent a person from slipping either into a scrupulosity, whereby he thinks he is a total wretch and unworthy to receive our Lord in the Holy Eucharist, or into laxity, whereby he thinks he has no sin, has hit the plateau of holiness, and thereby has no need for confession. For instance, during the 1600s, a very pessimistic, rigorous, scrupulous spirituality arose in the Church called Jansenism, influenced by the teachings of Luther and Calvin. These Jansenists thought the human condition was wretched due to Original Sin, required harsh penances to mortify the flesh, and deemed themselves incapable of making a good confession and unworthy of receiving Holy Communion.

On the other hand, in our more recent times, laxity is the problem. Too many people either do not know the difference between right and wrong or reject outright the moral teachings of the Church, relegating the Ten Commandments to mere suggestions. Too many people have lost a consciousness of sin, particularly serious mortal sin. Also, too many people neither understand nor appreciate the efficacy of the sacrament of Penance. Admittedly, part of the problem is that too many priests have neglected to preach about the importance of the sacrament. In sum, there is little wonder why so many people receive Holy Communion yet a fraction avail themselves to the sacrament of Penance.

Just like an annual physical exam with one's physician is a good, healthy practice, at least an annual (preferably monthly) examination of conscience is a good, healthy spiritual practice. Of course, this should not just be a cursory examination of conscience, but with the help of a guide (even an "app"), a thorough and sincere examination, which then leads to a good confession and sacramental absolution. With the soul renewed in grace, one can then be strengthened through the Holy Eucharist.

Finally, this precept is the minimum standard. Even though a person may not be in a state of mortal sin, regular confession of venial sin helps the individual to form his conscience better, fight against temptation, be aware of the occasions of sin, and progress in the life of the Holy Spirit (cf. *Catechism*, no. 1458). Pope Benedict XVI taught:

> In our Christian life, we must always aspire to conversion and that when we receive the Sacrament of Penance frequently the desire for Gospel perfection is kept alive in believers. If this constant desire is absent, the celebration of the sacrament unfortunately risks becoming something formal that has no effect on the fabric of daily life. If, moreover, even when one is motivated by the desire to follow Jesus one does not go regularly to confession, one risks gradually slowing his or her spiritual pace to the point of increasingly weakening and ultimately perhaps even exhausting it. (March 17, 2008)

Regular confession is the recipe for sainthood, and all of the saints of our Church not only knew it but advocated it. Saint Teresa of Calcutta and Pope St. John Paul II both went to the sacrament of Penance at least weekly, because they were so in love with the Lord that they were mindful of the smallest violation of that love and did not want even the least venial sin to impair their relationship.

Therefore, as we begin the Easter celebration, the questions arises, "Have I made a good confession since Ash Wednesday?" If not, do so, and receive the abundant graces of our Lord who suffered, died, and rose for our salvation. As Pope St. John Paul II taught, "It would, therefore, be foolish, as well as presumptuous, . . . to disregard the means of grace and salvation which the Lord has provided and, in the specific case, to claim to receive forgiveness while doing without the sacrament which was instituted by Christ precisely for forgiveness" (*On Reconciliation and Penance*, no. 31).

Ascension

Forty days after Easter, the time had come for our Lord to return to his heavenly Father. As we profess in the Creed, "He ascended into heaven and is seated at the right hand of the Father. He will come again in glory to judge the living and the dead and his kingdom will have no end." The saving act is complete: In the mystery of incarnation, Jesus, true God, became also true man, elevating our human nature to an even greater one than that given to Adam and Eve. He perfectly revealed God's truth and love. He humbled himself to share in our humanity so that we could share in his divinity. By his sacrifice on the cross, he has freed us from sin, and by his resurrection, he has conquered suffering, death, and evil itself.

Now, having spent forty days with the apostles after Easter teaching them and preparing them for their mission, he ascended. With the Ascension, our Lord opened the gates of heaven and prepared a place for us in heaven, as he promised. We too will share in his resurrected glory. As we read in the Gospel of St. John, Jesus said, "Do not let your hearts be troubled. You have faith in God; have faith also in me. In my Father's house there are many dwelling places. If there were not, would I have told you that I am going to prepare a place for you? And if I go to prepare a place for you, I will come back again and take you to myself, so that where I am you also may be" (Jn 14:1–3).

Moreover, Christ is no longer bound by time and space: He is not locked into a particular place and point. Rather, he is with us, each of us, at every moment of our lives. As we pray throughout the psalms, Jesus, the Good Shepherd, walks with us, takes us by the hand, and leads us safely through the verdant pastures and even the dark valleys in this life, and one day he will lead us to everlasting life to the home of the heavenly Father.

Keep in mind that the Ascension is not simply an ending followed by a pause waiting for the return of the Lord. In the Gospel of St. Matthew, Jesus gave them the Great Commission: "All power in heaven and on earth has been given to me. Go, therefore, and make disciples of all nations, baptizing them in the name of the Father, and of the Son, and of the Holy Spirit, teaching them to observe all that I have commanded you. And behold, I am with you always, until the end of the age" (Mt 28:18–20). Filled with the Holy Spirit at Pentecost, the apostles went out to continue the mission our Lord. For example, St. James the Greater went to Spain; St. Thomas, to India; and St. Peter, to Rome. They all would be true witnesses—even accepting martyrdom, although St. John would survive the means of execution. (Remember the word *martyr* means "witness.") These apostles laid the foundation for our Catholic Church, which exists to this very day because Christ is with the Church, he is with each one of us, and he has prepared a place in heaven for us if we remain faithful. Therefore, through faith, hope, and charity, and the power of the Holy Spirit, we are not bound by the concerns of this time and space; we have our eyes fixed on Jesus and our hearts set on heaven.

Therefore, the Ascension gives us great hope. However, it also challenges us. We too, each in our own way, by virtue of our own baptism and confirmation, are called upon to share in the mission of Christ: to be a faithful witness and to make disciples. In preparing to celebrate Pentecost in ten days, take time to reflect on this challenge and the realistic ways in which you, too, can "answer the call."

Signs of the Times

In the Gospel of St. Mark, at the Ascension, Jesus also said to the apostles, "Signs will accompany those who believe: in my name they will drive out demons, they will speak new languages. They

will pick up serpents [with their hands], and if they drink any deadly thing, it will not harm them. They will lay hands on the sick, and they will recover" (Mk 16:17–18). Certainly, we cannot discount the supernatural graces that would enable a disciple to fulfill these miraculous signs: In Acts of the Apostles, St. Paul exorcized demons, and the apostles spoke in tongues, preaching the Gospel to foreign people. Both St. Peter and St. Paul cured a paralyzed man. St. Paul was bitten by a snake but did not die. A pagan priest of the goddess Diana tried to poison St. John but failed. All of the apostles must have been granted a facility to learn new languages as they preached throughout the Roman Empire.

We too have to be a sign of the times, even though we may not demonstrate such miraculous signs. Nevertheless, we can preach the Gospel message in such a way that is not only authentic but also vibrant and relevant, showing that the truth gives freedom and real love. Therefore, we have to preach in *new languages*. Living in a world of science and technology, which offers many goods, a person could be seduced into thinking, "Science has given me all the answers. I have control. Who needs God?" The faithful disciple does not discount science and technology but sees that it all points to God, who created with wisdom, design, and purpose. Pope Benedict XVI wrote:

> The more we know of the universe, the more profoundly we are struck by a Reason whose ways we can only contemplate with astonishment. In pursuing them, we can see anew that creating Intelligence to whom we owe our own reason. Albert Einstein once said that in the laws of nature "there is revealed such a superior Reason that everything significant which has arisen out of human thought and arrangement is, in comparison with it, the merest empty reflection." In what is most vast, in a world of heavenly bodies, we see revealed a powerful Reason that holds the universe together. And we are penetrating ever deeper into what is smallest, into the cell and into the primordial units of life; here, too, we discover a Reason that astounds us. (*"In the Beginning. . .": A Catholic Understanding of the Story of Creation and the Fall*)

We can *cure the sick* by showing the human compassion of our Lord's sacrificial love. In our society, life has become cheap and disposable, especially for the unborn, the disabled, and the elderly. Yet, Christians look upon every person with dignity and respect.

This is why we have Catholic hospitals, nursing homes, schools, and orphanages. I think of the good work of the Little Sisters of the Poor, who care for anyone, and keep prayerful watch when a person is dying. Recently, a priest friend of mine died of cancer; he had been cared for so lovingly by the Little Sisters. I know many families who have cared for elderly relatives or disabled relatives. Here is the witness of hope. Here is what attracts someone to believe.

We can handle serpents and withstand poison, in the sense of resisting and refuting the falsehood and error spread by the modern intelligentsia. When our Lord hung on the cross, the chief priests and elders said, "Let him come down from the cross now, and we will believe in him" (Mt 27:42). Many today say, "Lower the standard. Do away with the doctrine. Become relevant and then we will believe." Some say, "Christians are intolerant," when those who preach "tolerance" are intolerant, even violently so, of those who hold different beliefs. As Pope Benedict XVI so frequently taught, a dictatorship of relativism is exercised with the logic of power; that is, those in power will impose their beliefs on others. Let us also not forget that Lenin first coined the term "Political correctness" and purged anyone who disagreed with him.

We, however, are not called to dumb down our faith but to live the fullness of faith. If we did dumb it down, we would become so relevant we would be irrelevant. Yes, a Christian can be tolerant in that we treat all people with dignity and respect, but a Christian must not accept what is not true. We must not let our minds be poisoned and our faith paralyzed. Jesus is the standard, and we live by the higher standard of the cross. In so doing, we will show people true love, the justice, the peace, the freedom, and the joy from that standard.

We can *drive out demons*. Many people are possessed by their past mistakes, failures, and sins. They are possessed by hurts that they have faced in life. The devil always wants us to remember these things so as to ruin the blessedness of the present. But with Christ, we preach forgiveness. Through the sacrament of Penance, our Lord forgives, heals, and strengthens a soul. Through a person's act of forgiveness of others, he can place a limit on evil and begin to heal. As St. Augustine said, "We leave the past to the mercy of God, we live the present in God's love, and we look to the future trusting in God's providence." By living our faith, we can be the instruments who help others come to confession and be reconciled.

Therefore, as we pray at Mass, we await in joyful hope for the coming of our Savior. We go forth to be witnesses of that hope in this world.

Pentecost

Fifty days after Easter, the apostles and our Blessed Mother were gathered in "the upper room" in prayer, the same room where our Lord had celebrated the Last Supper and where he had appeared on the night of Easter. Ten days had passed since the Ascension. At the Last Supper, our Lord had promised that he would ask the Father to send the Holy Spirit, whom he called the Advocate, the Paraclete, the Spirit of Truth. The Holy Spirit would make a dwelling within them. He would remind them of what our Lord had taught, instruct them, and enlighten them. And he would be with them always (Cf John 14).

Suddenly, a driving wind filled the room. Tongues of fire came down upon them. The Holy Spirit had descended. It was like Jesus and the heavenly Father together had exhaled and breathed on them, filling them with grace and the gifts they needed to continue the mission of the Lord and to found the Church, the same Catholic Church that we have to this day.

Interestingly, for the Jewish people, Pentecost (fifty days after Passover) was the anniversary of the giving of the law to Moses and the covenant. It was also the Feast of Weeks, celebrating the first fruits of the grain harvest. Here we see a fulfillment through the work of the Church: Christ made the new, eternal covenant, fulfilled the law, and bestowed the gift of finest wheat, the Holy Eucharist. The Preface for the Mass of Pentecost summarizes the meaning of this celebration: "For, bringing your Paschal Mystery to completion, you bestowed the Holy Spirit today on those you made your adopted children by uniting them to your Only Begotten Son. This same Spirit, as the Church came to birth, opened to all peoples the knowledge of God and brought together the many languages of the earth in profession of the one faith."

Gifts of the Holy Spirit

As we celebrate Pentecost, we need to remember that we too have received the life of grace and our identity of being a Christian and a member of the Catholic Church beginning at our baptism. Through the sacrament of Confirmation, we have received the fullness of the gifts of the Holy Spirit.

Now here is a challenge: Can you name the gifts? There are seven. So let's reflect, briefly. First, **Fear of the Lord**. Fear here is not servile fear, but a reverential, holy fear. We love God above all things. God is God. He is our top priority. We make time for God. Therefore, we worship at Mass on Sunday and pray daily, even when doing so involves sacrifice.

Because of our reverential and holy fear of God, we see the evil of sin. We fear committing a sin, not just because of the just punishment for sin and the fires of hell, but because we offend God whom we love above all things. Such reverential and holy fear makes us contrite and moves us to repent, confess, and be reconciled.

Second, **Piety**. We appreciate the fact that we are children of God, Christians, and members of the Catholic Church. As part of

this spiritual family, we love as a child loves, with tenderness and devotion. This is why we genuflect before the tabernacle, make the sign of the cross very reverently, or kiss the crucifix. We also realize that all of our blessings come from God, and we are grateful for them.

Fear of the Lord and Piety are connected with the supernatural virtue of **Hope**, whereby we trust in the promises of God for the help of his grace, the forgiveness of sins, and everlasting life. The virtues of **Temperance** and **Justice** are also empowered by these gifts.

Third, **Knowledge**. We receive and accept the faith. We believe in what God has revealed and what our Church teaches. Moreover, we know what is of God—what is true, good, and beautiful. So, when looking at the beauty of creation, a person may well appreciate the findings of science but should also come to know an omnipotent, omniscient, and good God who designed it all, gave it purpose, and gave life. When facing a moral decision, we know what is true, good, and right in the eyes of God. When discussing issues, we have a spiritual intuition whereby we can say, "I know this does not sound right."

Knowledge also enables a person to see everything in relationship to God and his eternal destiny: We know we will face sufferings and trials, but we see them in light of the cross. We know they will bring us closer to the Lord, and they have value, especially when offered for the Poor Souls in purgatory or the reparation of our sins or of others. Also, we not only know that this life will come to an end but also know that if we remain faithful, by his grace, we will share everlasting life.

Fourth, **Understanding**. Having faith, we have a deeper insight into the sacred mysteries, like the Holy Trinity or the Holy Eucharist. With understanding, we can better live our faith and explain it to others.

We also can discern and understand God's will for us. This understanding could be prospective, as when discerning a vocation: "Am I called to the priesthood or religious life?" This understanding could also be reflective, as when looking back on one's life: "I understand now how this event—even though a real trial—was to my benefit." The supernatural virtue of **Faith** is connected with the gifts of Knowledge and Understanding.

Fifth, **Counsel**. Counsel enables us to make good decisions: we examine a situation, discern right from wrong, consider the best course of action, and think of consequences (because a good action may have disastrous consequences). We can also counsel others and help them make the right decision. Counsel, too, is connected to the supernatural virtue of **Faith** and empowers the virtue of **Prudence**.

Sixth, **Wisdom**. The gift of wisdom enables us to think with the mind of Christ as St. Paul teaches. This virtue is linked with the supernatural virtue of **Charity** because it gives a loving and intimate knowledge of God. We appreciate divine things, we see the work of God in our lives, and we set our hearts on what is truly important. The more we share our life with the Lord with knowledge and understanding, the deeper the wisdom.

Seventh, **Fortitude**. We have the courage to live our faith and to persevere, even when we face trials, hardships, temptation, persecution, and, yes, even martyrdom. Remember Jesus said that the Holy Spirit is the Advocate, who will be with us and enable us to speak even when we may not have the words. Fortitude is connected with the supernatural virtue of **Charity** and the virtue of **Fortitude**.

Pray for the Holy Spirit to enkindle these gifts with the fire of his love. We cannot simply shelve the gifts. For example, if a person gave me a new car, I would think, "What a great gift!" But what good is the car if I kept it in the garage and never drove it? The same is true here. The Holy Spirit fills us with these great gifts at Confirmation, but we have to enact them in our lives. The beauty is that if we do, they will produce fruit: charity, joy, peace, patience, kindness, goodness, generosity, gentleness, faithfulness, modesty, self-control, and chastity (see Gal 5:22–23).

We must also be on guard; St. John warned us to test the spirits: "Beloved, do not trust every spirit but test the spirits to see whether they belong to God" (1 Jn 4:1). There is the spirit of evil—the

Devil—also known as Satan, the Murderer, the Prince of Darkness, and the Father of Lies. We see that spirit at work: Instead of Fear of the Lord, presumption: "I can live the way I want to without any thought of God and still get to heaven." Instead of piety, arrogance: "I deserve to receive Communion; I can leave Mass after Communion instead of waiting for the blessing; God should be thankful I am here." Instead of knowledge, intellectual pride: "I will decide what is right and wrong. I know more than the Bible and the *Catechism*." Instead of understanding, confusion: "How could God do this to me? How could this happen to me?" Instead of counsel, relativism: "Do whatever you want; there is no right or wrong; what is right for you, is right for you." Instead of wisdom, pride: "It is all about me." And, instead of fortitude, cowardice and vacillation.

As there are fruits of the Holy Spirit, there are fruits of the spirit of evil: St. Paul warned us as much, "Now the works of the flesh are obvious: immorality, impurity, licentiousness, idolatry, sorcery, hatreds, rivalry, jealousy, outbursts of fury, acts of selfishness, dissensions, factions, occasions of envy, drinking bouts, orgies, and the like. I warn you, as I warned you before, that those who do such things will not inherit the kingdom of God" (Gal 5:19–21). Yes, we see the spirit of evil at work in our world.

So this Pentecost, we must pray for an outpouring of the Holy Spirit in our lives, our homes, our Church, our country, and the world:

> *Come Holy Spirit, fill the hearts of your faithful and kindle in them the fire of your love. Send forth your Spirit, and they shall be created. And you shall renew the face of the earth. O God, who by the light of the Holy Spirit, did instruct the hearts of the faithful, grant that by the same Holy Spirit we may be truly wise and ever enjoy his consolations, through Christ Our Lord. Amen.*

Why Be a Catholic and a Member of the Catholic Church?

Pentecost challenges us to reexamine our own faith and our role in the Church. So ask yourself the following questions: "Why am I a Catholic? Why do I belong to the Catholic Church? How well do I bear witness to my faith and help in the mission of the Church?" These are important questions especially, though not exclusively, for young people. First, because our Christian identity is constantly challenged by the politically correct secular paganism of our society. Second, because too many Christians are more like smoldering embers than burning flames; they have been baptized, they may even go to church, but their faith is not alive. They say they are Christians, but they live like pagans. And third, because the second largest Christian "denomination" in the United States consists of lapsed Catholics.

Being on fire with the Holy Spirit and having received the fullness of his seven Gifts at Confirmation, each of us ought to say, "I am a Catholic because I believe in and I love Jesus as my Lord and Savior, and I believe in and love what the Catholic Church is all about." Why should we answer this way?

First, Christ directly and intentionally founded the Catholic Church. Any good historian must admit that the first Christian Church existing since the time of Christ is the Catholic Church. In Acts of the Apostles (11:26), the early believers were known as Christians, distinct from the Jews. Around the year AD 100, St. Ignatius of Antioch used the word *catholic*, meaning "universal," to describe this one Christian Church. The first major break in this one Catholic Church occurred in the year 1054 when the patriarch of Constantinople excommunicated the pope, and the pope responded in kind, thereby giving rise to the Orthodox Churches. In 1517, Martin Luther sparked the Protestant Reformation, really a revolution, which, for example, rejected and denied the Mass as a sacrifice, the sacrificial priesthood, the efficacy of sacraments, transubstantiation, purgatory, and the authority of the pope. Luther also removed seven books of the Old Testament. Today, there are numerous Christian denominations, from those original few of the 1500s to over thirty thousand other denominations today. Nevertheless, the one Church that Christ directly founded is the Catholic Church. This does not mean others cannot go to heaven; they can, but it does mean there is something very special about the Catholic Church. Therefore, the Second Vatican Council taught that the fullest means of salvation subsists within the Catholic Church (*Lumen Gentium*, no. 8).

Second, Christ entrusted his authority to the apostles, the first bishops. He gave a special authority to St. Peter, the first pope and first bishop of Rome. This apostolic authority has been handed down through the sacrament of Holy Orders from bishop to bishop, and then by extension to priests. Any list of popes begins with St. Peter. Any bishop if possible could trace his Holy Orders back to one of the apostles. My dear friend Bishop William Curlin, now deceased, had a calligraphy which had his name at the top, and then who ordained him as bishop, and back and back until the Middle Ages; if the written records had been available, the line of succession could have been traced back to the apostles and ultimately to Jesus. How good it is to know that the leadership authority of our Church is founded on the apostles, not Parliament, not a convention, and not a particular priest or minister or personality!

Third, Christ, who is the Way, the Truth, and the Life (see Jn 14:6), entrusted his teaching authority to the Magisterium, the living teaching authority of the Church. The Holy Spirit, whom our Lord identified as the Spirit of Truth, guides the Magisterium to

preserve, understand, defend, and teach God's truth. Yes, God's truth is found in Sacred Scripture, the written Word of God inspired by the Holy Spirit which teaches firmly, faithfully, and without error those truths necessary for salvation. Remember that it was the Catholic Church that decided to accept the forty-six books we call the Old Testament and to accept the twenty-seven books we call the New Testament, which together we know as the Bible.

This truth is also in Sacred Tradition, meaning the handing on and the teaching of the faith guided by the Holy Spirit, whom our Lord said would teach us everything and remind us of everything that he had taught. The Holy Spirit protects the Church from teaching error in faith and morals. For instance, everything we state in the Apostles Creed and Nicene Creed is true; these creeds were formulated to present a clear teaching of what we believe. The Church also teaches on current moral issues—like nuclear war, organ transplants, and euthanasia—so we can live an authentic Christian life today. The *Catechism of the Catholic Church* is a beautiful example of the handing on and the teaching of the faith since the time of the apostles.

Therefore, the Bible and Sacred Tradition form the deposit of revelation; that is, truth. Although, we live in an age where many scoff and say, "What is truth?" like Pontius Pilate, God is true. His revealed truth is universal and absolute. God's truth is inseparable from his love. With his truth and love, we can live in justice and freedom. We are blessed to have a teaching authority so we can live authentic Christian lives and live in freedom as children of God.

Fourth, Christ gave the Church seven sacraments which give grace to strengthen us on our journey through life. For example, at Mass, we offer a living sacrifice that participates in and makes present anew Jesus's sacrifice. Unleavened bread and wine are transubstantiated into his Body, Blood, Soul, and Divinity. Christ is truly, substantially present in the Holy Eucharist. We receive Christ into our lives. In all, through the sacraments, we share in our Lord's holiness and grace and are prepared to share in his life fully in heaven.

Fifth, Christ is with his Church. Yes, over the centuries we have faced persecution, schism, scandal, and human frailty, but the Church continues because Christ the Risen Lord is with the Church. In every day and age, no matter how dark the times, there have been great saints who have shone brightly through the darkness. During their lives, the saints gave a heroic example of faith, but they also continue to guide, inspire, protect, and pray for us today. Think also of those faithful Catholics who have handed on the faith to us and have helped us believe. Yes, we are sinners; that is why we pray at Mass, "Lord, look not on our sins, but on the faith of your Church." The Church, despite the frailty of its individual members, carries on the mission of Christ.

The challenge for each of us then is to be on fire with the Holy Spirit and filled with his breath, not only to live the faith but also to spread the faith. Like St. Paul said, we must be witnesses that we are children of God and believers in the Lord Jesus. Yes, there are those forces that would like to suffocate us or extinguish us, but they will never succeed. The Risen Lord is with us. The Church will always survive.

Therefore, as we celebrate Pentecost, we will put away our paschal candle that has burned in the sanctuary all Easter. Think though of how many candles we could light from it—an infinite number. The fire and breath of faith must now be passed on through us. We must be instruments to ignite the faith in others. We must go forth and renew the face of the earth!

Postscript

I hope and pray that you have found this collection of traditions and stories, meditations and spiritual activities useful for your Easter preparation and celebration. Moreover, I hope they lead you to a deeper appreciation for the beauty of our Catholic faith. In his Easter Message of 2009, Pope Benedict XVI, said, "From the depths of my heart, I wish all of you a blessed Easter. To quote St. Augustine, 'The resurrection of the Lord is our hope.' With these words, the great Bishop explained to the faithful that Jesus rose again so that we, though destined to die, should not despair, worrying that with death life is completely finished; Christ is risen to give us hope." Therefore, I hope and pray that this collection will help all of us rejoice in the hope which our Lord and Savior, Jesus Christ, has won for us through his passion, death, and resurrection. As the early Christians proclaimed to one another on Easter morning, "Alleluia! Christ is risen! He is truly risen!"

About the Author

Father William P. Saunders was born on March 9, 1957 in Washington, DC, to Dr. Joseph F. and Pauline C. Saunders. In 1959, his family moved to Springfield, Virginia, where he was raised. He has one older brother, Joseph F. Saunders, Jr.

After graduating from West Springfield High School as the class valedictorian in 1975, he attended the College of William and Mary, Williamsburg, Virginia. He graduated in 1979 with a Bachelor of Business Administration degree in Accounting and with membership in Beta Gamma Sigma Honor Society.

During the summer after college graduation, Father Saunders focused on the vocation to the priesthood, with which he had been wrestling since college. He applied to the Diocese of Arlington, Virginia, for admission into the seminary and was assigned to St. Charles Borromeo Seminary, Philadelphia, Pennsylvania. In 1984, Father Saunders graduated from St. Charles Seminary with a Master of Arts in Sacred Theology, *summa cum laude*, and was ordained to the Holy Priesthood on May 12.

As a priest, Father Saunders has served as the Assistant Pastor at St. Mary Catholic Church in Alexandria, Virginia (1984–1988), the Campus Chaplain and Adjunct Professor of Theology for Marymount University, Arlington, Virginia (1988–1993), the Assistant Pastor (1993–1995) and subsequently the Pastor (1995 to 2000) at Queen of Apostles Catholic Church in Alexandria, Virginia.

During this time, Father Saunders pursued studies at Catholic University, receiving a Doctor of Philosophy in Education Administration in May 1992.

He was appointed as President of the Notre Dame Institute for Catechetics in 1992, a graduate school offering a Master of Arts in Catechetics, Sacred Scripture, and Spirituality. On February 1, 1997, the Notre Dame Institute officially merged with Christendom College, Front Royal, Virginia, becoming the Notre Dame Graduate School. At that time, Father Saunders was appointed Dean of the Graduate School.

In Summer 2000, he was assigned as the founding pastor of Our Lady of Hope Catholic Church in Potomac Falls, Virginia, where he continues to serve. In Fall 2018, Bishop Burbidge appointed Father Saunders as the Episcopal Vicar for Faith Formation, overseeing the religious education and evangelization programs for the Diocese of Arlington.

From 1993 to 2006, Father Saunders wrote a weekly column entitled "Straight Answers" for the *Arlington Catholic Herald*, the diocesan newspaper. In 1998, he published a book by the same title, *Straight Answers*, and in 2003, a second volume, *Straight Answers II*. To mark the dedication of Our Lady of Hope Church and School, he published *A Labor of Love* in 2008. He continues to write periodically for the *Arlington Catholic Herald* and other publications.

In 2018, his book *Celebrating a Merry Catholic Christmas* was published by TAN Books.

Bibliography

The information in this book represents my thirty-four years of preaching and teaching. Some of the most prominent sources include the following:

Butler's Lives of the Saints. Notre Dame, IN: Christian Classics, 1956.

The Catholic Encyclopedia. New York: The Encyclopedia Press, Inc., 1914.

Cirlot, J. E. *A Dictionary of Symbols.* New York: Philosophical Library, 1962.

Cruz, Joan Carroll. *Eucharistic Miracles.* Rockford, IL: Tan Books and Publishers, Inc., 1987.

Customs and Traditions of the Catholic Family. Long Prairie, MN: The Neumann Press, 1994.

Fisher, Celia. *Flowers and Fruit.* London: The National Gallery, 1998.

Emmerich, Anne Catherine. *The Dolorous Passion of Our Lord*

Jesus Christ. Rockford, IL: Tan Books and Publishers, Inc., 1983.

The Eucharistic Miracles of the World. Bardstown, KY: Eternal Life, 2009.

Gall, Dom Roberrt Le Gall. *Symbols of Catholicism*. New York: Assouline, 1996.

Hahn, Scott, ed. *Catholic Bible Dictionary*. New York: Doubleday, 2009.

Klein, Peter. *The Catholic Source Book*. Orlando, FL: Brown-ROA, 2000.

Levering, Matthew. *Christ's Fulfillment of Torah and Temple*. Notre Dame, IN: University of Notre Dame Press, 2002.

Matford, J. C. J. *Dictionary of Christian Lore and Legend*. London: Thames and Hudson Ltd., 1983.

McKenzie, John L. *Dictionary of the Bible*. New York: Macmillan Publishing Co., Inc., 1965.

New Catholic Encyclopedia. Washington, D.C.: The Catholic University of America, 1967.

Pitre, Brant. *Jesus the Bridegroom*. New York: Image, 2014.

Ratzinger, Joseph. *"In the Beginning . . ." A Catholic Understanding of the Story of Creation and the Fall*. Huntington, IN: Our Sunday Visitor, Inc., 1990.

———. *Dogma and Preaching*. San Francisco: Ignatius Press, 2011.

———. *Jesus of Nazareth: Holy Week: From the entrance into Jerusalem to the Resurrection*. San Francisco: Ignatius Press, 2011.

————. *Jesus of Nazareth: The Infancy Narratives*. New York: Image Books, 2012.

Sheen, Fulton J. *Life of Christ*. New York: MacMillan Publishing Co., 1958.

————. *The World's First Love*. New York: McGraw-Hill Book Company, Inc., 1952.

Sri, Edward. *A Biblical Walk through the Mass*. West Chester, PA: Ascension Press, 2011.

Weiser, Francis X. *Religious Customs in the Family*. Rockford, IL: Tan Books and Publishers, Inc., 1956.

Image Credits

p. vi: *The Fall of Christ on the Road to Calvary*, Garnier, Etienne-Barthelemy, Restored Traditions.

p. vii: *Ascension of Jesus* (1845), oil on canvas, Faber, Christoffer. Public domain via Wikimedia Commons.

p. 3: *Incense during procession on Easter week in Antigua Guatemala*. Photo by David Paniagua Guerra, Shutterstock.

pp. 4–5: *Old rosary and ash - symbols of Ash Wednesday*. Photo by Joanna Dorota, Shutterstock

p. 6: *The Fight Between Carnival and Lent* (1559), oil on oak, Pieter Bruegel the Elder. Public domain via Wikimedia Commons.

p. 9: *Pancakes for Shrove Tuesday*. Photo by Ivana Lalicki, Shutterstock.

p. 10: *Christ in the Wilderness* (1872), oil on canvas, Kramskoi, Ivan. Public domain via Wikimedia Commons.

p. 12: *Moses and the Burning Bush*, with Moses Removing His Shoes (ca. 1465), oil on panel, attributed to Dierick Bouts the Elder.

p. 13: *Ash Wednesday*, Paris, France. Photo by Godong / Bridgeman Images.

p. 18: *Woman with Cross on Forehead in Observance of Ash Wednesday*. Photo by berni0004 / Shutterstock.

p. 20: *The Angelus* (1857–1859), oil on canvas, Millet, Jean-François. Public domain via Wikimedia Commons.

p. 23: *Family Saying Grace Before Eating*. Photo by Monkey Business Images / Shutterstock.

p. 27: *Giving Alms* (1900), Lamme, Ary Johannes. Public domain via Wikimedia Commons.

p. 30: *Beer and salted pretzels on wooden background*. Photo by Anna_Pustynnikova / Shutterstock.

p. 33: *Three Monks and a Snack* (1885), oil on canvas. Grützner, Eduard von. Public domain via Wikimedia Commons.

p. 34: *The stations of the cross at Maméan, in the Maumturks in Co. Galway, Ireland*. Photo by Sharonlflynn. Public domain via Wikimedia Commons.

p. 37: *Christ Meets His Mother while Carrying the Cross*, Caravaggio. Restored Traditions.

p. 40: *A confessional of St. Peter's Basilica in Rome, Easter Sunday Painting by Emile Ernest Hillemacher* (1818-1887) 1847 Paris, Musee d'Orsay. Photo © Photo Josse / Bridgeman Images.

p. 45: *Kneeling Woman at the Confessional*. Photo by PIGAMA / Shutterstock.

p. 47: *The Penitent Magdalene* (ca. 1635), oil on canvas, Reni, Guido. Public domain via Wikimedia Commons.

p. 51: *Moses Descends from Mount Sinai with the Ten Commandments* (1662), Bol, Ferdinand. Public domain via Wikimedia Commons.

p. 56: *Saint Joseph with the Flowering Rod*, oil on canvas, Guercino. Public domain via Wikimedia Commons.

p. 61: *Childhood of Christ* (ca. 1620), oil on canvas, Honthorst, Gerard van. Public domain via Wikimedia Commons.

p. 63: *The Death of St. Joseph* (18th century) oil on canvas, Altomonte, Bartolomeo.

p. 68: *Saint Joseph with the Infant Jesus* (1620s), oil on canvas, Reni, Guido. Public domain via Wikimedia Commons.

p. 76: *Door or screen from a church organ; the Annunciation to the Virgin Mary; Angel Gabriel* (oil on panel), Bonsignori, Gerolamo, Museo del Castelvecchio, Verona, Italy; Bridgeman Images.

p. 79: *The Annunciation* (1528), oil on panel, Tisi, Benvenuto. Public domain via Wikimedia Commons.

p. 84: *Our Lady of Sorrows*, 1509-1511, central panel of the altarpiece from the Mother of God church, by Quentin Massys (1466-1530), oil on panel. G. Dagli Orti /De Agostini Picture Library / Bridgeman Images

p. 88: *Bouquet of Roses at the Window* (1832), oil on panel, Waldmüller, Ferdinand George. Public domain via Wikimedia Commons.

pp. 92–93: *Triumph, Passion, Crucifixion and Resurrection concept*. Photo by Muskoka Stock Photos / Shutterstock.

p. 94: *The Entry into Jerusalem* (15th century), Master of the Thuison Altarpiece. Public domain via Wikimedia Commons.

p. 98: *The Accursed Fig Tree*, illustration from 'The Life of Our Lord Jesus Christ', 1886-94, Tissot, James Jacques Joseph, Purchased by Public Subscription / Bridgeman Images

p. 100: *Judas Iscariot: Betrayal of Jesus to the Sanhedrin for Thirty Silver Coins* (engraving), Tarker / Bridgeman Images.

p. 104: *Chrism Mass in San Giovanni Laterano, P. Villanueva*. Public domain via Wikimedia Commons.

p. 109: *Oil of Catechumens. Holy Wednesday. Chrism Mass, Meaux, France*, Godong / Bridgeman Images

p. 112: *Detail from the Last Supper*, Ghirlandaio, Domenico, Photo © Nicolò Orsi Battaglini / Bridgeman Images

p. 115: *The Last Supper* (ca. 1562), oil on panel, Juanes, Juan de. Public domain via Wikimedia Commons.

p. 118: *Last Supper of Christ mosaic outside a Catholic church in Germany*, photo by Hadrian / Shutterstock.

p. 121: *Eucharist, Holy Communion*, photo by Cavee / Shutterstock

p. 125: *Ostensory for worship at a Catholic church ceremony*, photo by Sidney de Almeida / Shutterstock

p. 129: *Altar of the Eucharistic Miracle of Lanciano*, photo by Luca Aless, public domain via Wikimedia Commons.

p. 132: *Christ Crucified with Virgin Mary, St John, and Mary Magdalene*, Van Dyck, Restored Traditions.

p. 135: *Christ in the Garden of Gethsemane* (ca. 1753), oil on canvas, Tiepolo, Giovanni Battista, public domain via Wikimedia Commons.

p. 137: *Flagellation of Christ*, Bouguereau, Restored Traditions.

p. 138: *Crowning with Thorns*, Caravaggio, Restored Traditions.

p. 142: *The Descent from the Cross* (1889–1890), oil on canvas, Fugel, Gebhard, public domain via Wikimedia Commons.

p. 147: *Christ Carrying the Cross* (1590–1595), oil on canvas, El Greco, public domain via Wikimedia Commons.

p. 152: *Monument to St. Dismas in Austria*, photo by Manfred Kuzel, public domain via Wikimedia Commons.

p. 155: *The Confession of Saint Longinus*, illustration from 'The Life of Our Lord Jesus Christ', 1886-94, Tissot, James Jacques Joseph, Purchased by Public Subscription / Bridgeman Images.

p. 157: *Saint Veronica*, Costa, Restored Traditions

p. 159: *Pietà con Nicodemo e Giuseppe d'Arimatea* (ca 1495), oil with tempera on panel, Perugino, Pietro, public domain via Wikimedia Commons

p. 160: *Christ Falling on the Way to Calvalry*, Raphael, Restored Traditions.

p. 163: *Hot Cross Buns*, photo by Shebeko / Shutterstock

p. 164: *Christ's Descent into Limbo*, Tintoretto, Jacopo Robusti, Cameraphoto Arte Venezia / Bridgeman Images

p. 169: *Traditional Polish Easter Baskets with Food - Holy Saturday, Easter Eve in Poland*, photo by SylwiaMoz / Shutterstock

p. 172–173: *Easter Mass at Saint Peter's Basilica*, Godong / Bridgeman Images

p. 174: *Great Vigil of Easter Saint-Gervais France*, Godong / Bridgeman Images

p. 179: *Original Score of The Messiah*, Handel, George Frederick, Coram in the care of the Foundling Museum, London, Bridgeman Images

p. 180: *Marble Grave Depicting a Liturgical Calendar for Easter, for Years 532-626*. Byzantine Civilization, 6th Century. © A. Dagli Orti / De Agostini Picture Library / Bridgeman Images

p. 183: *The Three Marys at the Sepulchre*, c.1684/85 (oil on canvas), Baciccio, Il (Giovanni B. Gaulli), Bridgeman Images

p. 186: *Woven Dish with Pysanky, Ukrainian Easter Eggs*, photo by Andriana Syvanych / Shutterstock

p. 188: *Easter Lilies in Church*, photo by ChiccoDodiFC / Shutterstock

p. 194: *Ascension of Christ*, Jouvenet, Jean Baptiste, Restored Traditions.

p. 197: *Icon: Ascension of Christ with the Hetoimasia*, tempera on panel, Ritzos, Andreas, public domain via Wikimedia Commons.

p. 198: *Saints Peter and John Healing the Lame Man* (1655), oil on canvas, Poussin, Nicolas, public domain via Wikimedia Commons.

p. 202: *Pentecost II*, Maino, Juan Bautista, Restored Traditions.

p. 205: *The Holy Spirit*, photo by BrankaVV / Shutterstock

p. 211: *Christ Giving the Keys to St Peter*, Peter Paul Rubens, Restored Traditions.

p. 214: *Easter Morning* (1818), oil on canvas, Overbeck, Johann Friedrich, public domain via Wikimedia Commons.

p. 216: *Easter Cross Covered in Flowers* (1872), lithograph, Whitney, Olive E., public domain via Wikimedia Commons.